LAWYER

MY TRIALS AND JUBILATIONS

LAWYER

MY TRIALS AND JUBILATIONS

JOE JAMAIL

WITH MICKEY HERSKOWITZ

EAKIN PRESS Austin, Texas

A NOTE ABOUT SOURCES

The bulk of what appears in these pages is based on the personal experiences and files of Joseph D. Jamail, Jr. Additional research ranges from published works, to newspaper articles from the *Houston Chronicle* and the *Houston Post,* to legal archives.

Material in Chapter 5 is reprinted with permission from *America's Top Trial Lawyers,* by Dr. Donald E. Vinson, Prentice Hall Law and Business.

Material in Chapter 7 is reprinted with permission from *Oil and Honor: The Texaco-Pennzoil Wars, by Thomas Petzinger,* Putnam.

FIRST EDITION
Copyright © 2003
By Joe Jamail
Published in the United States of America
By Eakin Press
A Division of Sunbelt Media, Inc.
P.O. Drawer 90159 ⌨ Austin, Texas 78709-0159
email: sales@eakinpress.com
🖥 website: www.eakinpress.com 🖥
ALL RIGHTS RESERVED.
1   2   3   4   5   6   7   8   9
1-57168-809-9
Library of Congress Control Number: 2003111085

Typography and design by Amber Stanfield

To the best jury a husband, father, and lawyer could possibly have, Lee and the boys, Dahr, Randall, and Rob, without whose love and support none of my trials and jubilations could have happened.

CONTENTS

When I decided to put on paper a great part of my life, I questioned the reason for doing so. It finally became obvious to me.

I have spent most of my life dealing with sorrow, pain, and problems. The hours ran into weeks, then months, then years—many years.

It is a great burden to take on the responsibility of helping people who have, through no fault of their own, lost their independence, the ability to earn a living, the pride of being able to provide.

The only thing most working people have is their health, which they use to work and support their families. When this is taken from them, more than a paycheck is forfeited.

I have listened to and watched children who have been blinded and mutilated; adults who have been brain damaged, burned, maimed. It is very emotionally draining, because I become involved with each of them—and there have been thousands.

They touch me, and I touch them. I have done my best to restore some measure of lost dignity, at least monetarily, by helping them to provide. And by letting them know that within the legal system there are those who care.

To those who would belittle and denigrate these people by restricting their rights, I say, have they no sense of justice, no decency? Shame on all of them.

ACKNOWLEDGMENTS

I want to express my appreciation to all who ever worked with me, who brightened my days and in various ways are part of this book, most especially:

Denise Davidson, my longtime aide, advisor, secretary, general in charge of this firm and, mostly, my friend.

Janet Hansen, for not only being a very fine lawyer, but helping me get ready to try cases and expertly trying them with me.

Frank Staggs, for his many years of especially fine lawyering. He is considered by me, and by most knowledgeable lawyers, as one of the best appellate lawyers in the state of Texas.

To Darcy, Jana, Artie, Melva, and sweet Elisha for their unwavering loyalty and caring. And a few of the special people who were formerly with me—Carolyn Borque, Diana Kelso, and Robin Young, who worked with us for eight years and still works with us as a structured settlement expert.

No one has a better personal staff, and no one can do this alone. I know I can't.

And finally, my friend Mickey Herskowitz, who in his unique way prodded and pulled until I would tell this in my way.

And if in these pages it seems that most of those mentioned are described as my very dear friends, most are, for I have been blessed with too many to mention. They know who they are, and the great enjoyment and comfort they have brought me, and how they enriched my life. I have tossed out crumbs and gotten back a bakery. (As a general exception, the people I exclude from the list of friends are those who owned or defended companies I sued.)

Down Home with Texas'
$10.5 Billion Barrister

By Steve Coll

Houston, Texas
July 31, 1986

There is no dearth of stories to tell about Joe Jamail, the Texan and self-described "sore-back lawyer," who this morning will defend in state appeals court here the astounding $10.5 billion verdict that marks the zenith of his mind-bending, muckraking career.

There's the story about his first big case, where his client was driving drunk one night, jumped a curb, and hit a tree—and Jamail sued the city for putting the tree in his way, and won.

And there's the story about how Jamail chose his profession. It has to do with a certain "well-endowed bar lady" Jamail fell in love with some years back at the Buckhorn Bar in Lafayette, Louisiana, and how, while he was busy mooning over her, an attorney named Kaliste

Saloom (honest) managed over a dozen whiskeys to convince him that the practice of law "was a pretty good racket."

Of more recent vintage, there is the tale about how on the night before closing arguments in *Pennzoil v. Texaco*—the case that led to the unprecedented $10.5 billion award last fall—Jamail was holed up in his immense house, writing, when Lone Star legends Willie Nelson and Darrell Royal, ex-football coach at the University of Texas, happened by in a white stretch limousine. After a few moments of mad pounding on the door, Jamail let them in.

"They kept me up all bleeping night long drinking," Jamail says. "An' I go over there the next morning to court bleary. Now that's how you get ready to argue a case."

Which brings us to a story behind the Willie Nelson record hanging on Jamail's office wall. One night after Nelson had finished recording it, he played it for Jamail and Jamail told him, "Willie, this bleep will never sell." After *Stardust* sold millions, Nelson framed his platinum album and sent it to Jamail with a note that read, "You're right, Lawyer."

There are these stories, and many more. String them all together and what you have is a book, or maybe a movie starring Dustin Hoffman. Which reminds Jamail of another story.

"Denise!" he shouts to his secretary. "Who was that writer for Dustin Hoffman? Well, anyway, he spent about ten days with me and I told him, 'Look, I don't want to be in the movies. I don't want to do any of that bleep, please.' Bleep that, man, I got to try lawsuits. I enjoy tryin' lawsuits, and I want to keep doing that."

Jamail leans forward in his brass rocking chair.

"Blee-eeeep!"

"You're gonna have to edit me," Joe Jamail announces

first thing in the morning, and the shame of it is, he's right.

The problem is not merely that Jamail rarely utters a sentence fit for publication in a family newspaper. Nor is it simply that the stories he likes to tell about himself and his compatriots in the plaintiffs' bar tend to stray into impolite subject matter.

The real trouble is that Joe Jamail has spent a lifetime calculating the effect of his outrageous words on ordinary people—the sort of people who sit in jury boxes and pass judgment on his clients. And thus he has developed an acute self-consciousness about his own charisma. He is that rare person who understands the source of his power over others.

This is not to imply that Jamail is phony. No man could feign the life he has led—raw, fervent, uninhibited. Jamail's favorite word for all things off kilter is "goofy," and it is an apt description of himself. It has the right tone: effervescent, buoyant, crazed, but redeemable.

And yet there are deceptive contradictions about him. Most obviously, there is something cold and steely and lethal lurking beneath Jamail's glowing facade. "Cute lawyers have never had much success with me," he says, "because I can get deadly serious." In trial, it will happen during cross-examination, when Jamail senses nervousness or fear in a witness and bores in until, as one of his colleagues puts it, "there is blood on the floor." Away from trial, his ebullience yields instantly to gravity if offense is given.

For example: It's early on a weekday afternoon, and Jamail has wandered over to the federal court building a few blocks from his corner office, amid downtown Houston's clot of steel and glass towers. A friend, and fellow personal injury trial lawyer, has asked Jamail to give expert testimony as to the appropriateness of a $500,000 fee the friend is seeking in a bankruptcy case.

Without compensation, Jamail has agreed to testify that half a million dollars is a fair price for his friend's services.

But the hearing is a fiasco. The judge is forty-five minutes late and, when she finally arrives, neither she nor the lawyers seem prepared to dispense with the day's business. At first, Jamail sits happily in the back row of the courtroom, regaling an audience of young attorneys with jokes and stories about the hemlines of certain cocktail waitresses and stewardesses he has known. Later, after the hearing drags on far longer than Jamail has anticipated, he mutters sourly, "This is what happens when lawyers get paid by the hour."

Finally, after nearly an hour of testimony and before Jamail can be called to testify, the judge shuts down the hearing and orders the whole matter postponed until next month (the lawyers have failed to notify all the parties about the hearing, she says). The lawyers storm into the hallway, furious—and also embarrassed that they have wasted Jamail's valuable time. They vent their wrath on the judge in a series of angry one-liners until one of them finally bursts out, joking wildly, "For $500 you could have her blown away!"

Jamail has been strangely silent amid the others' laughter. Now his words cut sharply through the hallway: "Don't even joke about that. It's a felony." His anger is awkward but intense, and he excuses himself to visit with a friend down the hall. Later, he explains that the judge is a friend, and he was uncomfortable with the spirited criticism of her competence.

The incident passes quickly; within a few minutes, Jamail is grinning mischievously again. He has fetched his black 1986 Jaguar from the garage and is cruising the downtown streets, headed for his afternoon session of two-fisted drinking at the Four Seasons Hotel bar.

He used to have a chauffeur, he says, but the man

rarely got a chance to drive. He points to his speedometer and explains why he likes his new sports car: When the gauge reads 150 MPH, you can lay your foot down on the accelerator and watch it creep to 160.

Age and alcohol, the perennial foes of a trial lawyer, have taken little toll on Jamail, who at sixty-one displays more stamina and energy than many attorneys half his age. He eats carefully. And he talks as if his life will never end. Explaining that in his youth he almost made a career of teaching history, Jamail says matter-of-factly, "I had enough hours to get my master's. All I lacked was writing my thesis. I'll go back and do that someday."

When and whether Joe Jamail teaches children history depends, at least in part, on the final outcome of *Pennzoil v. Texaco,* the case that rocked the American financial community and last fall brought one of the country's largest corporations to the brink of a bankruptcy filing.

The lawsuit arose from a protracted and deeply contentious takeover battle that began about three years ago among Pennzoil Co., Texaco Inc., and Getty Oil Co. A series of internal disputes between Getty Oil management and Gordon Getty, son of the late tycoon J. Paul Getty and the company's largest stockholder, put Getty Oil "into play," as Wall Street describes a company ripe for acquisition. Pennzoil, led by CEO J. Hugh Liedtke—a longtime Jamail friend—allied itself with Gordon Getty and made a bid for control. After an extraordinary twenty-five-hour Getty Oil board of directors meeting, Pennzoil thought it had a deal. But a few days later, Texaco stepped in at Getty Oil management's invitation and bought the whole company.

Liedtke, the rejected suitor, was devastated. Ever since his early days as George Bush's partner in the Texas oil patch, he had been trying to build a major oil company, and Getty Oil would have put him over the top.

"I have never seen him as hurt," Jamail says. "He

doesn't feign to me. Just one on one, there wasn't anybody taking pictures or anything. And he let it out . . . He couldn't make himself come to grips with the fact that somebody in the oil business running a large oil company was going to do things like this. Now this may sound corny to you, but I'm telling you how it came across. It's the only reason I got in the case—or, one of the important reasons."

After a series of legal maneuvers and preliminary successes, Pennzoil brought its case against Texaco (it sued for "tortious interference with a contract") to Houston, where it could be tried before a jury, and where Jamail, known locally as the King of Torts, would be in his element. On a fishing trip with Liedtke in Arkansas, just a few weeks after the case had been moved to Houston, Jamail was finally persuaded to take it on.

"Do you still want to do this?" he asked Liedtke one day on their boat.

"Yeah."

"I'll do it. Let's go get a drink."

The trial was wild and angry. Jamail decided that the way to win was to "keep it simple." So he tried at every turn to transform what might have been a muddled, boring contract case into a sweeping morality play—an indictment of takeover practices on Wall Street, generally, and of New York lawyers and investment bankers, in particular.

The turning point, many of the jurors said afterward, was Jamail's cross-examination of Martin Lipton, a name partner in the prominent New York law firm of Wachtel Lipton Rosen & Katz, and perhaps the best known takeover lawyer in the country. In the Getty takeover deal, Lipton represented the J. Paul Getty Museum, which controlled a crucial swing block of Getty Oil shares. Jamail relentlessly attacked Lipton's personal credibility, and he soon had the well-spoken lawyer tongue-tied.

The question-and-answer the jurors remembered most vividly, the one they could recite verbatim when the four-month trial was finished, was an exchange that drove to the heart of the case as Jamail presented it:

"Mr. Lipton," Jamail asked after his adversary had been on the stand for hours, "are you saying that you have some distinction between just us ordinary people making contracts with each other and whether or not it's a $10 billion deal? It's a different standard in your mind?"

"Yes, indeed," Lipton answered.

One of the jurors, a Houston city employee named Jim Shannon, smiles broadly when he recalls the exchange. "And of course," Shannon comments, wryly, "Jamail is about as ordinary as Croesus . . ."

"I could smell it. I could smell it," Jamail says, eager to relive the scene. "I'm not saying he was frightened. He was nervous . . . See, early in the case I had said, 'They'll bring Marty Lipton in here.' And Jim Kronzer (a friend of Jamail's who worked on the case with him) bet me $500 they wouldn't bring him.

"When they brought him and put him on the stand, I just turned to Jim and said, 'Now. Pay. Right now.' I thought once I established with him that he was not going to be able to flimflam me with words, that he was not going to be able to make his speeches, which lawyers would like to do . . . I had him."

Says Lipton, who vigorously defends his role in the takeover but is reluctant to discuss publicly the specifics of his testimony: "Joe Jamail was clearly the dominant personality in that courtroom."

Richard Miller, the veteran Houston attorney who tried the case for Texaco against Jamail, says now that he did not want to call Lipton to the stand at all, but that he was forced to do so by his client.

"He was a potentially dangerous witness because the

other side had targeted him," Miller says. "I knew that. . . . They set us up. If Lipton hadn't come, it might have changed the lawyers' approach to the case."

Still, Jamail insists, "I don't think Marty Lipton lost that case. I just think that the facts beat them."

Whatever it was, Texaco was not just beaten, it was routed. The gargantuan judgment returned by the jury last November—more than five times as great as any other civil verdict in American history, and roughly equal to Texaco's net worth—sent Texaco reeling and launched Jamail on a romp of celebration that seems to have slowed only a little. The appeal process has a long way to go, but Jamail is unconcerned.

"Hugh Liedtke absolutely got a property stolen from him . . . I don't have to prove this but once. And I've done that."

Of the many outrages Texaco claims were perpetrated against it at the Pennzoil trial, the one most prominently reported has been the $10,000 Joe Jamail contributed to the election campaign of Anthony Farris, the first of two state court judges to preside over the case.

Jamail made the contribution months before the trial, and before Farris was randomly assigned to handle the case (six weeks before the trial's end, Farris stepped down for health reasons and was replaced by another judge). And yet the influence of Jamail's campaign contribution, on perceptions of the case, will never be eradicated. "The Texas Common Law Massacre," one East Coast newspaper called it.

Texaco and its lawyers, of course, claim that Farris was biased against them from the start because of his relationship with Jamail. Before the trial began, they tried to have Farris disqualified, and failed; now the issue of Farris' partiality is on appeal. Whatever the merits of Texaco's allegations, however, a larger point about

Jamail's political connections has been missed in all the hoopla about his $10,000 offering.

"Joe is a very capable trial lawyer, especially in personal injury cases," says his rival, Richard Miller. "But his great talent is his sense for human frailty. He's probably the most politically adept trial lawyer in the state."

What Miller implies by "politically adept" is that like J. R. Ewing, Joe Jamail has some kind of relationship with nearly everyone who matters in Texas jurisprudence. The point, then, is not that Farris is a special friend of Jamail's; the point is that Farris is unexceptional in that regard. Nearly everyone in Houston is a friend of Joe Jamail's. One can see something sinister in that, or one can view it as the natural result of a rich man's long and successful life in a politically loose Texas boomtown.

Either way, Jamail's connections are undeniable. During a morning meeting with a visitor in his office, he takes a call from Roy Cullen, of the locally renowned and immensely rich Cullen oil family. Jamail tries to persuade Cullen to help a friend land a job as president of the University of Houston.

His connections are rooted in time as well as politics, money, and friendship—his family's ties to the city of Houston are now multi-generational. His father, a member of the same family as (the late) Lebanese president Amin Gemayel, came to Texas from Lebanon at age twelve. He started with a produce stand in the old downtown Farmers' Market, married another Lebanese immigrant—a strong woman, Jamail says, who influenced him greatly—and a few decades later had built a chain of twenty-eight grocery stores, which he eventually sold to a national food company.

Jamail says his own effusiveness was not paternally inherited. "My father was a very stern man, self-disciplined till you cannot believe, but kind, warm, a good daddy. He'd knock the bleep out of you if you needed it, but he'd love you, too. We never wanted for anything. He was successful. He never really spoiled us rotten with material goods because he had a sense of values."

One thing his father did not have, however, was an appreciation for the practice of law. Even after Jamail had become hugely successful (his father died in 1985, after reaching his nineties), Jamail the elder remained blasé about his son's profession.

"I was 'boy' to him until he died," Jamail says, smiling. "When I was fifty, I was 'boy.' And he loved me. And he really was proud of me. He never got in awe of this bleep at all. He really didn't like this bleep I was doing, you know, suing businesses, being a sore-back lawyer (legal slang for a personal injury lawyer), and he was oriented the other way. So was my mother.

"He came to see me try one lawsuit one time over in the federal court. That was the only time. Walked away and I went home to have dinner with him that night. And Lee (Jamail's wife of more than thirty-five years—about whom, he says, Willie Nelson wrote "Good-Hearted Woman") met me there. And my father looked at me, and he says, 'I thought there was something to this law practice.'

"I said, 'What are you talking about?'

"And he said, 'I watched you in there. Maybe it's because I'm so close to you, but you didn't impress me all that much.'

"Bleep—I did the jury. Anyway, that's the way it kind of went with him."

A new generation of muckraking Jamails is about to be unleashed. Even if they never live up to their father's $10 billion reputation, they'll be sure to raise some bleep. You can see it in Dahr, the oldest, who wanders through his father's office in tattered corduroys and a plaid work shirt.

Joe Jamail wouldn't have it any other way. Despite his

leading role in the corporate drama of the Pennzoil case, he remains in deed and spirit an old-fashioned plaintiff's populist, ready to right wrongs and bring the greedy to their knees—for one-third of the booty, of course.

"I like to help people," he says emphatically. "Listen, I could hire out tomorrow to the business world. They come in here every day. Every day. Banks. Every bank in town has tried to get me. But why do that? I'm not into that. And I don't need any more money. I think people are by and large getting the shaft. . . . And what they need is good lawyers like me."

BOOK ONE

THE BAR NEVER CLOSES

*"You may write the nation's laws,
if you will let me write the nation's songs."*
—IRVING BERLIN

"Why not both?"
—JOE JAMAIL, 2002

CHAPTER 1

RAISING THE BAR

My law career began, as so many of them do, with a broken beer bottle. In two respects, the case would be more difficult than the Pennzoil-Texaco trial nearly forty years later.

To begin with, I had no idea how much to seek in damages, or what my fee should be. It had taken a world war to get me into the University of Texas law school, and for a time my professors feared it would take another to get me out.

I grew up in very secure surroundings. No one has been luckier. I had a stern but loving father and a beautiful, caring, attentive mother, three brothers, George, now deceased, Emile, and Bill, and a gorgeous sister, Florence.

My grandmother lived across the street. So did my uncle Jim, my dad's brother, and my aunt Emily, to whom I was especially close, and their family, my cousins, along with my uncle A. D. and aunt Liza, and Dad's sister, Aunt Jamilia, and still more cousins.

17

The neighborhood was filled with us—and we liked one another.

My parents and siblings and relatives, along with the nuns who were my teachers in elementary school, instilled in me a sense of security and duty. And I thrived on this nurturing because of the stark contrast with the other side of the streets.

I grew up loved. And I grew up fighting. I had to.

I was teased because my grandparents had come to Houston from Lebanon and were not accepted for some time. I resented it.

My father had fought with the United States Army in France during World War I, and he urged me always, in fact, demanded that I never back off from what is right. He and my mother made me understand that honesty and integrity, along with pride and self-esteem, were my most valuable possessions.

I had to fight because I was a Catholic and most of the boys in the neighborhood, other than the Jamail boys, were not. They teased me, pushed me, taunted me, so I fought—a lot. Most bullies don't have big vocabularies, so your talks don't last long. I didn't win them all, but they soon quit.

I'm still at it, in a different way. Bullies and snobs have always ignited in me the fire that smolders inside my soul. I have never been able to stand by and let someone take advantage or abuse another person not as fortunate. I have to go in and help. And win.

Because that is me—Joe—and there, in that narrow alley between being hugged and being pushed, is where my instincts were shaped.

When the Japanese bombed Pearl Harbor I was sixteen and finishing high school, with a chip on my shoulder the size of a manhole cover. I had trouble staying in school and resented authority, which was really a reaction to having people tell me what to do. I thought they were

hypocrites, the lot of them. My brother George had pre-
ceded me at St. Thomas and he had been all-everything,
the first student to letter four years in football. One of
the priests started in on me the day I enrolled: "Why
can't you be more like your brother?"

Well, hell, he was fifty-five pounds heavier, for one
thing, and better looking. He was older by four years, almost to the day.

Whatever anger was building up in me, for whatever
reason, I would carry into courtrooms for virtually every
case I tried. I had a sense of humor and mischief, but it
was that anger that served me well.

Since I was sixteen, my only option seemed to be go
on to Texas A&M and be exempt from the draft. Most of
the Jamail men had gone to A&M, which had a rich tra-
dition as a military school, a lonely, womanless place
known as "Sing Sing on the Brazos."

Before my brother George went off to the Navy and
flight training, he figured he would get my Aggie experience off to a good start. He gave me his senior boots to
wear with my ROTC uniform, and when I appeared on
campus I thought it strange when people saluted me and
picked up my bags.

Of course, I didn't know any better. When I found my
room, someone said, "You're in the wrong place. This is
the freshman dorm."

And I said, "Well, I'm a freshman." Then they took
turns whipping my ass. I hung around nursing my
wounds for two days, then hitchhiked to Austin, to the
University of Texas. I enrolled in pre-med, took five
courses, and the first semester made five F's. I only re-
gretted that I didn't squeeze out a D, so I could have
claimed that I spent too much time on one subject. I
spent most of my time sleeping. I was lost.

At that point, I left the university, forged the signatures
of my mom and dad on an enlistment form, had a druggist

notarize it, and joined the Marines. I had not quite turned seventeen.

Thus began a series of misadventures that threatened to spoil the whole idea of getting involved in this great and bloody outbreak of global temper. I had finally told my parents what I had done. My mother could not stop crying. My father, who had the face of a warrior-poet, looked at me and said, "Try to be a good soldier . . . if you can." Then he walked away.

I knew I had made a mistake shortly before the train pulled out of Southern Pacific Station in downtown Houston.

I survived boot camp in San Diego and had gotten a forty-eight-hour pass with a fifty-mile restriction. I was so homesick I headed back to Houston, a four-day trip by rail. When the train stopped in Yuma, Arizona, I had already violated the fifty-mile rule. I said, "This is bullshit, I'm taking off." The shore patrol picked me up before I could reach the city limits and stuck me in a drunk tank with a bunch of Indians from a tribe in Yuma. When they put me back on the train, I was shackled, kids were yelling at me, and they had painted a big yellow P (for "prisoner") on the back of my uniform.

I served my time in the brig and finished basic training. The night before we shipped out for the War in the Pacific, I heard a jukebox in a honky tonk playing the song "Red River Valley." I felt really depressed, a condition made worse once we left the dock, because I quickly learned that I was unsuited for sea travel. I started throwing up, at least partly out of fear, I suppose. I remember one sailor making fun of me, the big, tough Marine going to win the war for us, puking his guts out. I wish I could have taken my head out of the commode long enough to knock him on his ass. This went on for six or seven days, until we docked in Hawaii.

When the war ended, I had been overseas for twenty-seven months, and I made it back home in February of 1946, thinking I was going to be discharged. They mustered you out of the service on a point system, and I figured I had more points than MacArthur. In April, in Houston, I made the mistake of answering the phone. Some idiot executive officer had run across my personnel records and decided I owed the Marines more time. He noticed that I had guard duty one night, got drunk and drove a jeep into an officer's barracks. I received a deck court martial and was sentenced to thirty extra days of police duty. So I packed up and went back to San Diego.

Military justice at that time was similar to being tried in, say, Pakistan. This was another exposure to the legal system that reinforced in me a deeply felt empathy for society's underdogs, of which I was one.

I made up my mind to go over the hill but reconsidered when it was pointed out that my misdeed had occurred in wartime and I could be shot for desertion. By this time I was a sergeant. I lay around for thirty days in the Slop Chute (the post saloon), and when a recruiter asked me if I'd like to reenlist, I assured him, "Kiss my ass."

As I left the base on foot, a car pulled up outside the gate. Behind the wheel I recognized the familiar, boyish face of Jackie Burke, someone I had known since St. Thomas High. He asked me if I wanted a lift home, so I rode back to Houston with a fellow Jarhead, who would later wear a different kind of green jacket—for winning the Masters golf tournament. He won a hell of a lot more tournaments before he finished.

No criticism of the Marine Corps is implied when I say we were not meant for each other. I respect the Corps, its record in combat, the brave men it produced. I served in outfits so tough, Rambo would have been the cook.

But as for my own experience, I identified with Dizzy Dean, the great pitcher for the St. Louis Cardinals, who joined the Army at sixteen and served in the cavalry at Fort Sam Houston. There he had a job shoveling manure from the horse corral. An officer demanded to know when Dizzy was going to deliver manure for his flower garden, and Diz replied, "Right away, sir. You are number two on my manure list."

I came home ready to party, feeling, as many veterans did, that I was owed something, although I was not sure what. Some of my friends had not made it back. Joe Pat Lyons was killed in the Pacific, with the Marines. Leon Shepard and Bill Gregg, the closest friend I had, died in action. They were all kids from the neighborhood. The oldest was eighteen.

Years later, I had an encounter that brought back the strange feelings of those days. I was making a speech at San Jacinto Junior College, and a shy young girl approached me. "Mr. Jamail," she said, "Bill Gregg would have been my great uncle."

After I finally got home to stay, I went shopping for civilian clothes. You couldn't find a decent white shirt or a suit or much of anything. My father took me to Sakowitz, an upscale clothing store then in the heart of downtown Houston. Mr. Simon Sakowitz was walking by and stopped to say hello to my dad. Then he turned toward me: "Joe, how are you?"

"Fine, Mr. Simon." I was in my Marine Corps trousers and green shirt.

He remembered me as a good boy and hugged me, thankful that I had made it back. "You're a *mensch*," he told me, a Yiddish word I didn't know. I was pleased to learn that it meant a man, an important man. "We got to dress you up, boy," he said and led me to a back room, where he rummaged around and found five white dress shirts. I am not sure if someone too young to have been alive then can understand this kindness. You couldn't steal five white shirts! Ties, trousers, a suit. I came back the next day to pick up my clothes, newly altered, and Mr. Sakowitz wouldn't charge us a dime.

The Sakowitz family and the Jamails were friends, and they respected the fact that we had a large and close-knit family. Mr. Simon was just happy for my folks, relieved that my brothers and I were home safely. He wanted to do something for us. That was the way people were in the 1940s. We had grown up with a lot of security. We lived in a Jamail compound—cousins, aunts, and uncles all around each other in the neighborhood. Across the street, down the block, Jamails everywhere. The movie theaters were all downtown, the Loews and the Metropolitan side by side. D'Arcy's was the popular drug store. All the high school kids hung out there on Saturday morning. Prince's Drive-In had opened on South Main, with waitresses in short shorts that drew us in like metal shavings to a magnet. They were photographed for *Life* magazine.

After I finally got home for good from the Corps, I spent nearly every night at the High Hat Club dancing, getting plastered, and staggering into bed just before dawn. One morning I climbed into bed with what was going to be a very wicked hangover, and at 5:30 my father walked in, jerked the covers back, grabbed me by the shoulders, and said, "Wake up. You have to get out of here. You're worrying your mama. And I don't want to hear any bullshit war stories, because I fought in the big war, boy." He handed me $300 and pointed to a Buick parked in the driveway.

"Take that car," he said, "and if I was you I'd drive to New Orleans and think about what you want to do with your life." I was all of twenty years old.

My father was a big, powerful man, very handsome, with piercing blue eyes. I worshipped him, and I was not going to disobey him. I was glad to have the cash, though. I had blown my mustering-out money and my accrued overseas pay, totaling $2,500, some of it gambling in the Balinese Room and the rest on a good-looking whore named Ruby. The Balinese was then one of the ritziest clubs in America, built on a pier that extended a half-mile into the Gulf of Mexico, with a series of doors that would swing shut in the event of a raid by the Texas Rangers. By the time the Rangers reached the casino, gaming tables had been converted into dinner tables. Couples would be innocently eating and drinking off fine linen tablecloths. When the Galveston County sheriff was asked why he didn't close the club down, he replied, "Because they would not let us in."

On my way to New Orleans, I stopped off in Lafayette and checked in to a hotel, where the hot spot was the Buckhorn Bar. They had a bunch of Cajuns who talked funny and a big-titted bar lady, and I thought to myself, "This isn't a bad place to spend a few days." I met a lawyer named Kaliste Saloom who convinced me I should enroll at the University of Southwestern Louisiana, home of the Ragin' Cajuns.

One day I dropped in on Kaliste at his office. I hung out and watched him talk on the phone, telling people what he could do for them, and I asked him, "You get paid for this?"

He smiled and said, "Not bad, huh!" At that moment, I knew I wanted to be a lawyer. It had never really crossed my mind before that day in Saloom's office, but, after watching him, I figured I could do what he was doing, and it looked like a truckload more fun than getting up at 4:00 A.M. to sell bananas and tomatoes.

Not that I am knocking the grocery business. I wasn't wild about the hours, but you cannot imagine what it was like to be a young boy wandering through the Farmer's Market, soaking in the scent of the fruit and the sight of wood shavings spilling out of crates, curled like potato peelings. These were charmed moments.

I knew my father would be relieved that I had made

a decision about my future. There had been lawyers in his family two hundred years before I was born. I wanted to please him, to make him proud. I think I did. He was ambivalent about the law. On one level he disliked lawyers. The family owned a chain of grocery stores, and someone was falling down every day and suing them. Yet he was so proud when I got my degree, married Lee, and started a family.

Three or four months before he died, my dad told me I had brought honor to the name of Dahr Jamail, a name that dated back to the Crusades. He didn't flatter people.

By the end of the year, I was ready to go back to Austin, where nearly everyone spoke English. I persuaded my professor of classical literature to give me an oral exam in the Buckhorn Bar. He was a runaway drunk from somewhere in the East, and he asked me a few questions about Shakespeare. Then he said, "Okay, young man, you just passed the course with a B. The drinks are on you." I bought a round, hopped into my car, drove to Austin, and enrolled for summer school.

I bumped into Wally Bowles, one of my best friends all through high school, and we found an apartment and became roommates. The apartment was great, next to an alley where you could bring girls in and out.

Every Friday, the Falstaff Beer distributor would deliver to our door a quarter keg of beer. At one time we had the largest indoor collection of flies in the world. The malt apparently attracted them. We finally started keeping the keg outside.

This time around the Forty Acres, I fared much better. I wasn't much of a student, but I graded well in courses I liked, such as history, English, and literature. I studied during the day and drank beer and shot pool at night, but I stayed in school and managed to graduate.

History is a subject that has always captivated me. During those years many of the professors who taught history at the University of Texas were legends in their prime. Walter Prescott Webb and J. Frank Dobie made the people and events leap from the texts and come alive in our minds. Those courses and the teachers who taught them have stayed with me to this day, and I am indebted to them for firing a passion in me that has never waned.

The five F's on my record from my earlier tour at Texas were a deterrent to my plans for law school. I went to Dean J. R. Parten, who had been an Army major in the First World War, and told him my problem, explaining that I had left to join the Marine Corps. He looked at me and said, "My only nephew was killed in the Marine Corps. Let's go across the street and drink a Coke." He was about seventy, a revered figure on campus. He and Dean Click, like Dobie and Webb, were giants. I loved them all.

Dean Parten said something to the secretary as we walked by the registrar's office, and when we came back there were five drop-slips on his desk, back-dated to 1942. He signed them, and I enrolled in the University of Texas Law School in September.

It has been pointed out to me, more than once, that for someone who chose a profession steeped in procedure and protocol, I had little use for either. I talked my way into the law school without taking an entrance exam.

All of this would later seem a fateful arrangement because I soon met the girl I would fall in love with and marry. Lee Hage was enrolled at Incarnate Word College, in San Antonio, with my sister, Florence. She came home with Florence one weekend. I took one look at her and said, "Okay, okay," very mild and revealing for me.

Florence snapped, "You leave her alone." We were the closest of the siblings, and she knew I would hustle anything. She ordered me not to put any moves on her friend.

Lee was petite, with a quality about her that reminded you of Edith Piaf, the French songbird known as "the Sparrow." She was from Austin, where her father owned a chain of variety stores and real estate properties and was a very wealthy self-made man. He was extremely friendly and generous and, next to my own father and my uncle Jim, was the man who influenced me the most.

Some months later, on a Sunday afternoon, Lee happened to be at home in Austin on holiday and I had driven back after a rowdy weekend at the High Hat in Houston. I called and asked if she would like to have dinner and a movie. She thought about it for a full minute and said yes. Wally Bowles joined us, and we took her to the Avalon on the Drag, a favorite spot for Texas students. Those were the days when you could not buy a drink at a bar, and you had to bring your own bottle of liquor, usually in brown paper bags. The clubs provided the ice and mixers. Finally, we took her home.

The next day Wally said, "You got to quit going with that girl." I asked him why. He said, "She's a lush. She drank all our whiskey."

When I saw Lee I told her, "Wally says you drank all our whiskey and if that keeps up you'll have to pitch in." She was indignant and gave me a look that would cure head lice. "I have never had a drink of alcohol in my life," she said.

I was smitten. Lee graduated from college when she was nineteen. She became a speech therapist and was almost too good to be true.

So, of course, I quit calling. I had started to worry about getting too serious too soon.

A year passed, and Florence called to ask me to take her to dinner. She was in Austin for the wedding of Lee's sister. I said, "You got it, darlin'," and drove down to Lee's house, where she was a guest. I saw Lee sitting nearby. She looked away and I walked off.

I refused to take Florence to the wedding but agreed to accompany her to the reception. Then I saw Lee walking down the staircase of the Driskill Hotel with some guy, and when she got to the bottom step I grabbed her arm and said, "You're going with me."

I took her to Jake's Cold Hole, a place with a great little three-piece blues and jazz band. We sat and listened to the music. I drank beer because Jake's had beer so cold it was almost frozen. I like it that way. We sat, looked at each other, and just visited. Finally, she insisted she had to go back to the reception. We drove to the hotel. I walked her in and the same guy was standing there. I said to her, "I'll pick you up tomorrow at six."

I did, and that second night Lee said, "I have to ask you something. After going with you for a year, I don't hear from you for a year. What is this all about?"

I said, "I'll tell you. I started to care about you more than I wanted to, and I knew I wasn't ready to get married. Now I am."

She wasn't. It was after dating more than a year longer that she finally agreed. Now I tried to find Mr. Hage so I could tell him Lee and I were going to get married, and he kept escaping me. Her dad was suspicious of me and didn't think I was very serious.

I used to drop by and fetch Mr. Hage and we would go to Scholz's, drink beer, and have a good time. But a nice-looking girl would stroll by and I'd fool around. He spent his life raising his kids, and Lee was his baby and his favorite. Her mother had died when Lee was three, from complications during childbirth.

We were not permitted to have a church wedding, because Lee had no intention of converting to Catholicism, a requirement in those days. So, instead, we were married in the Women's Federated Home by a Catholic priest bribed by my father-in-law, and also an Episcopal priest because Lee was Episcopalian. It was August 28, 1949.

Now that I was a semirespectable married person, the time had come to take my studies seriously.

My freshman year, I had flunked torts, my eventual

specialty, which became a favorite anecdote in every story every interviewer and magazine writer later did on my undergraduate days. I could pick up what I needed with ease, but about my second year I turned it on. After I had completed my second year of law school, I was sitting around Hillburg's Bar drinking with some law students, who were bemoaning the upcoming bar exam. I called out, "Quit your whining."

One of them said, "Okay, mouth, we'll bet you a hundred dollars you can't pass that sonuvabitch."

I drove to Houston and found Billye Russell, the only lady lawyer on the admissions committee from Harris County, to give me a waiver of the declaration of intent to practice law. I didn't even know I needed that. She was amused and graciously agreed. I gave the waiver to Mr. Stanley, the clerk of the Supreme Court, on Monday morning. There were some courses that would be on the exam that I had not yet taken. Kenneth Woodard, the assistant dean of the law school, loaned me his notes on mortgages, and several other professors lent me theirs on courses I had not taken.

It was as if I had a wave of blockers running interference, leading me onward. I took the test and had to wait six weeks for the grades to be released. On the day they were due, my friends rushed over to the dean's office. I didn't bother. I knew I had busted the exam and was prepared to pay up the hundred dollars.

The law school policy was to not post the grades, and Dean Page Keeton's secretary, Mary Lou, refused to sneak the results to my pleading classmates. So, to end the suspense, I made my appearance and she slid a piece of paper across her desk. Her face blank, she said, "Sorry, Joe."

I picked up the slip and stared at the number on the paper: 76. The cutoff was 75. I had overtrained by one point! We gave Mary Lou the rest of the day off and she joined us for beer to celebrate.

Some days later, we were sitting in Tony's beer joint, near the Texas campus, still celebrating, when Dorothy, the barmaid, popped the cap off a bottle of Pearl Beer and the top chipped, gashing her thumb. She was squalling and squealing behind the bar as she wrapped her bleeding thumb in a dirty dishtowel.

Half a dozen of us were observing the scene and offering varying degrees of sympathy and advice, when we decided to sue the Pearl Brewing Company for making a defective beer bottle. Fate had sort of thrown us together, Dorothy, the bottle, and me, a lawyer unsullied by past experience.

I had passed the bar; now I would try my first case six months before I graduated. I filed suit, and Pearl Beer filed a motion that I had not heard of, among many. Soon we were in court, in Austin, opposed by a widely respected attorney named Mack DeGuerin. His two sons, Dick and Mike, would go on to successful careers of their own, mostly in the practice of criminal law.

The courtroom was packed with my law school chums, and they were trying hard to contain their excitement. I am just grateful that "the wave" had not been invented yet. The judge asked for my response to the plea of privilege—"What say you, counselor?"

I said, with sincerity, "Judge, I don't know what I'm supposed to say. What do you think I should say?"

I was not trying to be deferential. I was just lost. The judge said, "Well, Mr. Jamail, this is a plea of privilege," which meant the defendant wanted the case to be removed to San Antonio. Of course, the judge sized up the situation immediately and saw that I didn't know enough to be embarrassed. He looked at Mr. DeGuerin and said, "Mack, do we really need to go through this? Make an offer and let's settle."

DeGuerin said, "Your honor, I am not authorized to go above $500."

I was beside myself, all but blown away by this exchange. I thought, "Five hundred dollars for a cut thumb? What a country." But my basic instinct took over and I said, "Judge, I think a thousand would be much fairer."

His honor said, "Mack, go call your office and ask for $750 and we'll settle this right now."

As DeGuerin went to find a phone, I addressed the bench: "Judge, what should I charge?"

"Well, counselor," he said, trying not to laugh, "the usual attorney's fee is one-third of the settlement." To myself I said, "Whoooeee, that's $250 for half an hour's work. I believe I have found my life's calling."

I was suddenly a hero to my friends, who were still waiting to get their licenses, while I had been in front of a civil court judge. The downside was that I had to buy beer all night long. It was like getting a hole in one in golf.

There was one odd consequence of my having passed the bar several months early. Dean Keeton discovered that I had never taken the law school entrance exam. He called me to his office and asked, "How did you get in here?"

I told him the truth. I had just walked in and started going to class.

It was not conventional, my law school experience, but I hardly suffered for it. There were many professors at the University of Texas Law School who were considered among the giants of their field of law. I had several of those: Leon Green, George Stumberg, Clarence Morris, Gus Hodges, Dean McCormick, Judge Stayton, Charlie Myers, Corwin Johnson. And the longer I was out of law school, the more I came to respect and appreciate what I learned there.

After my graduation, Lee and I moved back to Houston and accepted an offer from what was then one of the city's largest and most powerful firms, Fulbright, Crooker, Freeman and Bates (later Fulbright and

Jaworski). I worked there for a long time, approximately twenty minutes.

This fierce-looking woman opened the office door and laid down a list of rules: "You will not sign any documents that leave this office. You will use this stamp. You will not this and you will not that." I played around with the stamp on my yellow pad, and while I was so engaged the hiring partner stopped by, Mr. Kraft Eidman. He asked how I was doing. I said, "I think we both made a mistake, but I'm going to fix mine."

Eidman nodded and said, "If you're going to quit, do it now, because if you stay you will buy a house, have a mortgage, and we'll own you." I was gone from there twenty minutes later. Kraft Eidman and I became great friends for the remainder of his life.

Houston was booming as the 1950s arrived, and no lawyer, if he could find the courthouse, went very long without a job. The wildcatter Glenn McCarthy had opened the Shamrock Hotel on St. Patrick's Day of 1949, at a cost of $21 million. Lee and I went to the celebration. It was the most chaotic scene I had have ever witnessed. The movie *Giant* did not do it credit. The city's population had surged during the war, when 40,000 came looking for jobs at the shipyards.

Between 1951 and 1953, Houston held these distinctions: It 1) led the nation in murders, 2) was voted the cleanest city in America, and 3) was taking in a quarter of a million dollars a year in royalties from eleven oil wells drilled at the city garbage dump. No city can match that record.

In October of 1953, the district attorney, Dan Walton, offered me a position on his staff as a felony prosecutor, and I leaped at it. Dan was civil, calm, low-keyed, a gentleman—not always qualities widely sought in a district attorney. That move began the most productive years of my career.

I was making $600 a month and there was rarely any money left over after paying for essentials. But Lee was totally supportive, working, teaching school. That was an exciting time in my life. Walton gave me all the freedom I could want and all the work I could stand. I picked two or three juries a week and tried dozens of cases. It was very different then.

I sharpened my skills in the best way a lawyer can, by learning from my mistakes. In this process, I was aided greatly by two remarkable judges, Spurgeon Bell and A. C. Winborn. Judge Bell had a brilliant legal mind and taught night classes at the South Texas College of Law. He helped tame the wild streak that always had been a part of my nature. He taught me the value of patience.

Winborn had been a great district attorney, the only ever to get a death penalty against Percy Foreman. He told me once, "Joe, when you walk in here it's like letting in sunshine. You have a way with language. Don't let anybody change you." For one year he allowed me to experiment, yet made sure that I stayed within the rules of procedure.

My instincts were being refined, but they had been there always, even as a child. In a fight I always went for the jugular because I wasn't big enough to go any other way. I learned that if a lawyer can command the courtroom and his presence commands the jury to look into his eyes and listen to his words, his client's chances of winning soar.

Judge Bell and Judge Winborn let me be me, whatever that was at that particular time. A lot of judges would not have been as generous. There were other judges who would be an influence on me, among them Tom Coleman, Phil Peden, and Peter Solito.

I started out with the same fears every young lawyer has: the fear of facing a jury, of having a judge dislike you, of forgetting to make the points you need to make.

The load itself, the pressure to keep the assembly line moving, kept the juices flowing. I loved the combat, the closeness of the space, which made nearly every step you took an act of theater. I loved tangling with the other lawyers.

You could not help but develop certain rivalries. I frequently went up against one attorney whose clients lost with such regularity that I called him a booking agent for the penitentiary. He was a big old boy with a beer belly that fell well below his waist. Once, fed up with my taunting, he turned to the jury and said: "Jamail doesn't care what happens in this case. He's on the county tit. He gets paid by the county, win or lose."

When he sat down, I looked at him for a minute or two, this self-contented moose, and then I rose and said, "He's right about one thing, gentlemen." (I need to interrupt this paragraph to point out that, in the early 1950s, there were aspects of the judicial system that cried out for questioning and change. For one, those juries did not have women on them.)

"I do work for the county," I continued. "I work for you. I am YOUR lawyer, and that is what I am trying to be, unlike my fat friend over there, who is like a cab driver or a whore, who is for hire by anybody."

Judge Winborn's jaw dropped, hard, and he told the jurors to disregard those remarks. I don't think they could.

I tried every kind of case—rape, incest, murder, mule sodomy—and knew I would have to move on after a year or two. There was a law in Texas against sex with animals. This poor man had been amorous with a mule. My only question on cross-examination was, "Sir, how long have you been going with this mule?" The jury gave him five years in the penitentiary. Before he was sent away I filed a motion with Judge Winborn to set it aside and dismiss the case. He teased me for two days and then did so.

I needed to have my own practice, to provide for Lee and our future children. I needed to grow as an attorney. While I felt no guilt about sending away violent offenders, Houston was a city not that long removed from its frontier, and the citizens tended to favor authority. This is still true, to a somewhat lesser extent, today.

This trend was reflected in a song written and made popular by the famous folk singer Leadbelly (Huddie Ledbetter), called "The Midnight Special":

If you ever go to Houston,
You better walk right,
You better not stagger,
You better not fight.

Sheriff Binford will arrest you,
He will carry you down.
If the jury finds you guilty,
You are Sugar Land bound.

The sheriff of Harris County, in the years from 1918 to 1937, was a lawman named T. Binford. Sugar Land was then the location of the state prison farm. Every so often, a trip takes me in that direction and I see the prisoners working in the fields, with the white "P" stenciled on the back of their shirts, and I would remember my few days in the brig as a raw, seventeen-year-old Marine.

And I remember the confused and indifferent student who flunked his course in torts. So I believe in second chances. I truly do.

Papa was handsome and strict, Mama pretty and witty. Marie and Joseph D. Jamail, Sr., on their wedding day, at Annunciation Catholic Church in Houston, 1921.

I was seventeen when I left for the Marines, sixteen when I forged my parents' signatures on the enlistment papers. Served from 1943 to 1946. Later, they adopted the slogan "The few, the proud."

Baine Kerr, who would survive World War II to become the president of Pennzoil, was wounded at Guadalcanal and carried off on a stretcher.

(Above) Willie Nelson said he had my wife, Lee, in mind when he wrote "Good-Hearted Woman." He got that right. (Top right) Our three sons, Dahr, Rob, and Randall. (Below right) One of the few things that lives up to its advertising is being a grandfather: from left, first row, Martha, Noah, Robert, Joe. Second row, Blanche, Lili Marie, Dylan, Justice.

CHAPTER 2

A TREE IN THE MEADOW

I happen to have a giant ego, an admission that will not shock my close friends or critics. I am not uncomfortable in saying this because the ego of man often gets great things done. The trick is to learn how to contain one's ego, not conceal it.

By the time I left the district attorney's office, in 1954, I felt inferior if I wasn't at the courthouse trying a case. I described myself as a "sore-back lawyer," and I meant it because those were the cases that came to me, people injured in car wrecks or on the job, railroad workers and longshoremen. No one wants to pay the medical bills or provide for a widow and her kids, much less compensate someone for the loss of pride and dignity that goes with the loss of a job. I had a flock of those cases. The longshoremen had my number taped above the pay phone in the union's hiring hall, where they went to hang their hooks.

Then, as now, there were the society lawyers and the Hollywood lawyers, having marquee lunches with their celebrity clients. I knew that was where the glamour was, but I didn't want lunch to be the highlight of my day. I wanted the conflict, the clash of wills and wits. I still feel that way. Throughout my career, I have taken my lunch to my office or the courthouse in a brown paper sack.

Your education doesn't stop, of course, when you go into private practice. I joined the firm of Fred Parks, along with my friend George Cire. Fred was an interesting character, born in the Indian Territory, every inch a self-made man, who had a free wheeling practice. He had a piece of the Moody estate case, and the death of Joan Robinson Hill, which inspired the best seller *Blood and Money.*

Fred wore a miniature rose in his lapel every day, was still shooting his age in golf at seventy-nine—he lived into his nineties—and was a collector of fine wines. Parks also attracted a lot of what were called "shaggy dog" cases, and George and I tried most of them.

Cire and I usually tried of these cases together, and he always put me in front, taking the second chair and handling the details. He was two years ahead of me in high school. We both played left guard on the football team, wound up in the Marines and the University of Texas Law School, and became partners. He went on to become a federal judge, after serving on the state and appellate courts. He died of pancreatic cancer in 1986, after battling with it for almost two years.

For the period he was ill, I virtually dropped out of any kind of social routine, avoided my usual haunts, and took a bottle of vodka to George's bedside in the late afternoon, and we would sit and drink, his vodka, mine Scotch. He made me shave him every morning, and I hated it. "I may cut your damned throat," I protested once, but he said quietly, "Go ahead. It's got to be better than what I'm going through."

The next day I brought a bottle of sleeping pills with me. As George was a devout Catholic, suicide was not an option. But I told him, "You don't have to do it. Just say the word, and I'll do it for you. I'll mix these pills in the vodka and give it to you."

He thought about it, then shook his head. George could not take an easy way out. We sat together, night after night, until the end. He was the best friend I would ever have, and when a writer once asked me what I learned from him, I answered, "The bastard taught me how to die." He never inflicted his pain on anybody. He was a helluva man, and he died with so much dignity.

We had left Fred Parks after one year, and were partners, in 1959, when I agreed to try a personal injury case called *Glover v. the City of Houston*. It became better known, in Houston legal lore, as "the Case of the Killer Tree."

When one's record reflects a pattern of success, there is the appearance of boasting if one refers to it. But as Harry Truman so famously said, when asked about giving his opponents hell, "I'm just telling the truth. If it feels like hell to them, so be it."

As a product of Catholic schools, I learned as a child not to veer from the truth because you get caught every time. The nuns would swat me with a ruler or a paddle or a belt for lying, cheating, or whatever I had done. It just didn't pay, and I learned this very early: If you stand up and tell the truth once, it becomes a habit, and the beating is not going to be nearly as bad as if you had been caught in a lie.

My mother had five children. She had a great sense of humor, and she recognized early that I was the one most different from the rest of the bunch. She loved me mightily, as mothers do, but she proved it by not discouraging whatever it was that made me a rebel. Just before Lee and I married, my bride to be asked her what kind of little boy I had been. She answered, "The kind of little boy I wouldn't let my other children play with."

So a confidence was instilled in me that surfaced repeatedly in this way: I could not resist taking a case that someone told me could not be won. No one I knew thought *Glover* was winnable. It seemed to be a simple case of a drunk driver hitting a tree and getting killed. The facts, and public opinion, seemed to be on the side of the tree.

Nearly everybody loved trees. Doris Day had a megahit record, a love song whose lyrics included the lines "There's a tree in the meadow, with a stream drifting by ... and on this tree I see the words 'I'll love you till I die.'"

But this wasn't some romantic tree in a field of lillies. It was a tree in the middle of a street, forming an island encircled by cement, along with a second tree in the same block. They were adjacent to the campus of Rice Institute, as it was known then, and many residents felt the trees gave the neighborhood a nicer ambience. The trees had been the source of countless accidents over the years, but were spaced in such a way as not to alarm anyone except the victims and survivors.

The rest of the facts were these: The Glovers had gone to a friend's house and the hostess had not eaten, had a headache. Mr. Glover headed for Youngblood's Fried Chicken at Fannin, just off Sunset Boulevard. Before he left the house, he had two pops of bourbon and a can of peanuts—this became important later.

He picked up the fried chicken, in the rain, and made a left turn off Fannin onto Sunset. His car jumped the curb, went nineteen feet, knocked down a "Keep Right" sign, went another twenty-two feet, and hit the tree, critically injuring Mr. Glover. He was rushed to a hospital, where the police finished their investigation. They drew blood and filed a report that showed he was intoxicated. He lived nine days and then died. He was sixty-three.

Mrs. Glover had taken this case to just about every known plaintiff's lawyer in town, and they had turned her down. A friend of mine at the Old Union Bank asked me if I would talk to her. All she really wanted was for the city to pay the funeral expenses.

The case caught my interest, and I agreed to pursue it. People thought I was either crazy or doing it as a publicity stunt. The guy was driving drunk on a rainy night and ran into a tree in the middle of the road.

But I kept coming back to the nagging thought, "Why was there a tree in the middle of the road?" It was a damned tree, not a signal light. I knew I could sue the city if the accident did not involve a government function. I sued them under the common law theory of maintaining a public nuisance and stuck the mayor, Lewis Cutrer, on the stand to explain the function of the tree.

The city's lawyers brought in their toxicologist, a man I had known when I was trying cases for the district attorney. They led him through all the hoops and felt secure in their basic overriding defense: The man was drunk.

But I heard the toxicologist describe how the doctor had been opening Mr. Glover's chest when he ordered the officer out of the room. He had no surgical mask, no gloves. He had taken the blood from Mr. Glover's stomach cavity.

"Does it make any difference," I asked, "where the blood comes from?"

"Of course," the toxicologist answered.

"Explain that."

"If the sampling came from the vein, you could say it was in the bloodstream and conclude he was drunk."

"Is it okay, then," I asked, "if the officer drew the blood from the stomach cavity?"

"Probably not," he said.

"Hold it," I said. "Hold it right there. Now, if a man ate a can of Planters Peanuts after consuming a certain amount of liquor, would that distort the finding?"

"Oh, very definitely," he said. "It would slow the alcohol getting into the bloodstream, so the test of the blood from the stomach is not a reliable gauge as to what, if any, effect the alcohol had on Mr. Glover at the time of the collision with the tree."

I had finished my cross-examination, and I am not sure if I knew then that this would be a breakthrough case for me. In one respect, a little personal history already had been made. This was one of two cases Lee would ever watch me try—it simply made her too nervous. On this day she was sitting next to George Cire on the front row.

Judge Tom Coleman had called a recess, and I had retreated to the men's room, where I usually go in any time of stress. With a packed courtroom waiting for my final argument, my zipper broke.

I was getting panicky, and I believe in a similar circumstance most young lawyers would have felt the same. I peeked into the hall, eased out the door, and sneaked over to the elevators, where I asked an operator if she had a safety pin. She gave me a suspicious look and said firmly, "Your fly is open."

I said, "I know that. Do you have a pin?"

She said no.

When I tried to sort of slink into the courtroom, Judge Coleman was glaring at me and every attorney on the other side was grinning like a hyena. Before the judge could say a word, I blurted out, "Your honor, I'm late. I'm sorry I'm late, but I've had an unfortunate accident and broken my zipper, and I hope it doesn't distract the ladies on the jury." The jury cracked up.

The broken-zipper fiasco may not have been the reason Lee stayed away from my future trials, but we didn't see her in the courtroom again until *Pennzoil*.

There were three women on the jury. This was when women had just begun serving on juries in Texas, and the press coverage across the country was wild. The jury came back and gave us everything we asked for, including a thousand dollars a day for pain and suffering, which at that time was unheard-of. The city had to cut down both the huge trees on Sunset Boulevard and I, Joseph Dahr Jamail, a certified, dues-paying liberal, began getting hate mail from tree huggers all over America.

But half the mail was congratulatory, and I knew the case had touched a nerve when I heard people arguing about it on talk radio. I was bombarded with requests for interviews. Most people labored under the impression that you can't sue the government, but you can. We proved it by winning every appeal.

I also received a letter from Clarence Morris, my original torts professor, who by then was teaching at the law school at the University of Pennsylvania. It was written on embossed stationery:

"I have read with interest the account of Glover versus the City of Houston. When you were my student in torts at the University of Texas, I told you that you would never make a lawyer, and I meant it."

The letter made me laugh out loud. Professor Morris was Jewish, about sixty, with a head as slick as a glass table, and was married to a beautiful girl much younger. All I can say is he was a terrific law professor and I cherished his honesty. As a first-year law student, I remember the conversation as vividly these many years later as the afternoon it took place.

He asked me what my parents did. "Grocery business," I said.

"I suggest you become a grocer," he said. "You are just taking up space here."

Out of respect for Professor Morris, I will forego any temptation to list a synopsis of those cases, out of thousands, that may have seemed interesting at the time. Instead, I have selected a handful that range across the spectrum of the law. I will not burden you with any further effort to explain why they were chosen, on the theory that readers, like jurors, should participate in the joys of discovery.

Professor Morris and I began corresponding, and he later told me that he was happy for me and very proud to have been my teacher:

Dear Joe,

A couple of days ago (a copy) of the Houston Chronicle for 12 October 1975 came into my hands. . . . The second paragraph quotes an interview between you and me in which I say you "were not gonna make it as a lawyer." The article continues to report that you just cut the sixteenth notch on your gun.

If you had told me you were going to practice with a gun, and with a football coach and a country music singer as an advisory team, I might not have made so rash a prediction. Of course, I'm glad you have done well. I am pleased to hear of the successes of former students.

Sincerely yours,
Clarence Morris, The Law School,
University of Pennsylvania

The professor was not impressed with the facts of my my "tree" case, but in a humorous vein, he was aware of my friendship with Darrell Royal and Willie Nelson, the famed Texas football coach and the legendary musician.

I finished writing after they left, at midnight.

THE ELECTRIC BILL

A brave man named Olin Robertson had both hands and a foot burned off because of a faulty electrical box. He was pouring a chemical into a well, using a perforator gun that operated on electricity. Just as he reached to pull the switch, he saw a spark and the box exploded.

Under the heading of small mercies, Olin was unconscious for most of the first day of his ordeal as he was rushed to a burn unit in a Houston hospital. The doctors worked frantically to treat his blistered skin and to save as much of his arms as they could for the artificial limbs he would need later. One can only guess at the mental and physical agonies he suffered in those hours when he was lucid, wondering how he could cope with no hands, no job, a pittance to live on.

This was in the early 1960s, and my task was to give him back his life. To do this, I first had to figure out what had caused this horror and who should pay for it. Then I had to develop a plausible claim that would get his case into court.

The case had come to me in a roundabout way, beginning with a sympathetic company lawyer who would not leave Robertson naked. His employer, McCullough Tool, had to their credit agreed to keep him on the payroll. But he had been sent to this job to a Texaco well, a company whose path I would cross again. Texaco's lawyer viewed the accident as a simple Workman's Comp case, and he wrote a check for $12,000 to this man, who had a wife and two kids and grim years ahead.

Robertson made only one modest request. "You know, they tell me this leg prosthesis is going to wear out in two years," he said, "and it costs $2,500. Can you arrange to let me have $2,500 extra for that?"

A very good person and a very good lawyer, and a friend, Finis Cowan called the Rig-A-Lite company, who had installed the equipment. He asked that company's attorneys to add another $2,500 to get a release and settle. Those dummies said no, we won't contribute a dime. So Cowan inserted language in the settlement that preserved Olin's right to sue; otherwise, the settlement would have released everyone. "You better get a lawyer," he advised him, "and pursue that."

And he did. The attorneys for McCullough Tool turned out to be two men I knew well, Judge Roy Hofheinz and Red James. Hofheinz was the visionary who built the Astrodome and had been a county judge at thirty. The two men were livid over the way the company had brushed off a man now crippled. They called me to ask if I would take the case, and I did.

I reenacted the accident, and it was clear to me that the cause was a little junction box that carried electricity the same way you plug a razor into a socket. My immediate problem was what to plead. Texas torts law, at the time, did not accept product liability. You had negligence or nothing. The box was ten years old.

I thought about it until my hair hurt, and I decided to gamble on making new law in Texas. I would hold the product manufacturer liable. The jurors would have to ask, Was the product safe at the time it was made and for the purpose it was intended? This was totally different from negligence. If they answered no, it was not or had not remained safe, was the product the proximate cause of the accident?

To my knowledge, a personal injury case had never been submitted that way before in Texas. It was a forerunner of the products liability law the state adopted. So this was the real legal significance of the case of Olin Robertson against Rig-A-Lite.

I had not invented this concept, of course. I am a hungry reader, and I had read that California was toying with the idea and thought, Why not here? I would not skip the plea of negligence, but would modify it so the main thrust of the charge was met, and create something different.

I studied the matter for days and weeks. Then the light came to me: The law is not just a straitjacket. As long as the theory is credible, as long as it is reasonable, the law does not prohibit me from being creative. Otherwise, the law would have stagnated and died a thousand years ago. The manufacturer should be liable for the reasonable life of a product.

The defense contended that the box was so far away from the electricals that it could not create an arc, which you had to have. That was what the industry bible, *Ohms Electrical Law,* said. My expert knocked down that theory. I said it was bullshit. If you couldn't challenge *Ohms,* if a manual was going to be the judge and jury, we didn't need a courthouse.

Olin told his story honestly and without self-pity. I didn't have him on the stand fifteen minutes. The jury knew the injuries were there, but you can't win on emotion. The judge instructs them not to be swayed by sympathy.

I was able to prove that the box had a faulty seal that did not adhere to the metal properly and allowed water to get in over a period of years. The box started to rust, which caused a short, which caused this man to lose his hands in a most horrifying way.

Still, it took a courageous judge, Bert Tunks, who was willing to submit it that way, who wasn't bound by some rule thirty, forty, or a hundred years old.

I told the jury, at the beginning of the case, I believed then and I still do, "If you can't decide this case in the amount of $510,000 in thirty minutes, then you need to tell the judge that you need to go on home." You have to challenge them, convince these ordinary people that they are big enough to stand up to this company. This has been my war cry before, during, and after the Texaco verdict. It has the added virtue of being true.

Rig-A-Lite's insurance company was defending the case, and their lawyers played for a hung jury. In twenty-eight minutes, the buzzer rang. Oddly enough, the company had a $500,000 policy, a fact unknown to me when we calculated the damages. With interest they were out another $80,000.

This was the first time in American tort law that a single individual was awarded $500,000. It took another eighteen months to start collecting the money. Olin bought a house he could get around in.

Let me be clear on one point. I don't set out to bankrupt companies. I don't get a kick out of that. But this is not an issue of law. Which is what Justice Brennan told the Texaco lawyers, in the Supreme Court of the United States, about the bond in the Pennzoil–Texaco case: "That is of no concern to us. The bankruptcy courts will have to deal with that."

You have to dare to take chances; otherwise nothing improves. After the verdict came in, Judge Tunks reversed the jury verdict, but he did not reverse the case. He entered a judgment—it was now 1965—for the defendant, which is called judgment *non obstante,* but that allowed me to appeal based on the jury's verdict and kept it all in focus. And the state Supreme Court upheld us. A year and a half later, Texas passed a products liability law. I'm proud of that.

I suppose that was the case that lifted me out of the provincial, small-market status. I began to get calls from all over America. The story went out on all the news wires, and *Newsweek* magazine ran an item on it: "A new King of Torts is Texas counsel Joe Jamail." Of course, it was ego building, and I do have to stay on constant guard against that demon.

If I let flattery dictate to me what cases I picked, I was going to wind up somewhere in Disneyland.

Life Is Like a Box of Chocolates

The legal profession is governed by a code of behavior at least as rigid as that accepted by doctors and not far behind the one observed by organized crime. Near the top of the list of ethics is this admonition: Never fall in love with a client.

I violated that restriction. When we met, she was fifty-one, weighed well over two hundred pounds, and was paralyzed, unable to move anything but her head and mouth and one hand, slightly. For most of her hours, she watched the world on her stomach, the position most comfortable to her.

On a rainy day in 1969, in Houston, her 1963 Chevrolet Impala crashed into a guard rail on the recently opened Pierce Elevated. Like a lot of large people, she leaned back when she came around a curve, and the steering wheel lifted up in her hands. The car spun out of control and hit the rail. Mrs. Williams' neck was broken.

The accident left her crippled for life and ended her career as a schoolteacher. She had been to several lawyers and none would take the case. They saw what General Motors saw: a black woman driving a car that was nearly seven years old.

What I saw was a woman with an irrepressible spirit and an amazing history. Her grandparents had been slaves. She had moved from Waxahachie to Houston and went to work for Miss Ima Hogg, the daughter of a former Texas governor and one of the city's foremost patrons of the arts and charities. Miss Hogg took a liking to her and insisted that she complete her education. Elnora finished high school and then enrolled in what was called the Houston Negro College, now Texas Southern University. Miss Ima's driver took her to and from the campus.

When she finally received her degree, she was a widow with three children, including two sons she put through college. One was a major in the Army, the other an official with Texaco. She also had a daughter who was retarded, and later she earned a master's degree at the University of Houston, in special education, to better cope with her daughter.

I decided to take her case, and Gus Kolius and I tried it in 1972, in front of an all-white, all-male jury. The argument caused a gasp in the courtroom and was quoted in several law journals and national magazines. "She didn't crawl in here," I said, "and she isn't crawling out. *She is no Aunt Jemima.* She is a human being. Either you are big enough to look at it that way or you're not."

Some people thought that reference was audacious, or even tasteless. But I forced them to look at her. She had no bandanna on her head, no flour on her hands, and no self-pity in her heart.

We had a mechanic named LaRue who testified that the carter pin that held the steering mechanism was apparently dislodged. General Motors brought in a team of engineers from their plant in Saginaw, Michigan—and you know GM can line up enough engineers to fill a stadium.

They had built a model of the chassis of this old Impala, and I proved that they spent about $35,000 making it. After they set up their exhibit in the courtroom, during their experiment the wheel wouldn't budge, not up or down, not even the slight adjustment the equipment was designed to make. Gus whispered to me, "We're screwed. It couldn't have happened the way we said."

But I had seen a reddish blush in the face of their chief engineer and I heard their lawyer stutter for just a moment. I thought, "There is something wrong here." So the first question was, "Are you funning with me and this jury and this court, or do you have a model here that is defective?"

The GM engineer couldn't speak for almost a minute. Then he said, "Well, it's frozen."

I said, "It's not working the way it is supposed to work. It's defective in this regard, isn't it?"

"Yes, sir. It's supposed to come back when you pull on it, but it's rusted into place."

I nodded. "And you took special care to hand make this model and you still couldn't get it right!"

I wouldn't let them remove the chassis from the courtroom, and every morning when I walked by I would turn and kick it. Gus had made the opening argument, and when I closed, I said to the jury, "You know, gentlemen, I don't know whether to lean over and kiss this chassis or kick it again."

After they deliberated, the jurors found the manufacturer liable for $1,551,620—half a million more than we had asked for. Judge Warren Cunningham reduced the award to a million dollars, plus interest. He would not let us make a trial amendment. GM's appeal reached the Supreme Court, where it was turned down without comment.

But even at the lower figure Elnora Spriggs Williams became the first black woman in America to receive a million-dollar verdict. She and I appeared in *Jet* magazine, the first time a white guy had been featured in the magazine's pages. We both broke the color barrier.

Hers was a wonderful and uplifting story, and I just fell in love with the lady. She called me once a month until her death, and she always said something to make me laugh. Every Valentine's Day I would take her a box of chocolates. They were her favorite, chocolates in the big red heart-shaped satin box.

A SILVER DOLLAR GOES FROM HAND TO HAND

There ought to be a special place in hell for people who abuse and take advantage of elderly widows. If I had my way, there would be some triple bunking going on in the case of three lawyers who all but picked clean a lady who was, in the 1970s, extremely vulnerable. Her plight received special attention because she happened to be the widow of a man larger than life in a city famous for them.

She was Alice Sneed West, whose husband was Silver Dollar Jim West, oilman, rancher, philosopher, gambler, and eccentric. When Jim West died in 1954, he left a fortune estimated at about $100 million. He had earned his nickname from his custom of giving away silver dollars, from a bag that was with him at most times.

He gave them away in the Depression, when Mr. Rockefeller was giving away dimes.

Jim West was no cartoon character. He was handsome, smart, and gregarious. When he built his house in River Oaks, the Houston Light and Power Company made him angry, and he built his own generator. It made so much noise that his neighbors complained they couldn't sleep. He also kept two hogs and two mules in his back yard. Jim was the cause of many of the restrictions that made River Oaks the most exclusive residential area in the city.

When his house was demolished in 1969, about $290,000 in silver dollars was found buried in the foundation. It was an impressive collection, but far short of the millions that were rumored to be there.

Mrs. West outlived her husband by twenty-four years and lived in lavish style, making frequent trips to Paris and Las Vegas, the latter to watch the performances of Elvis Presley and Dean Martin. Her great wealth, and her addiction to alcohol, made her an easy mark for scoundrels.

I heard all the colorful stories about Silver Dollar Jim West and once saw him coming out of the coffee shop at the Stephen F. Austin Hotel, reaching into his bag and tossing a handful of silver dollars in the air. People got on their hands and knees to scramble for them. This was in the early 1950s, and a dollar tip was a fine tip.

I never met West, but I respected his legend and his

refusal to let his riches wall him off from common people. And in what became a pattern in my career, I had met members of the family, which led to my taking one case, which led to another.

In the early 1970s, I heard from Bill Lloyd and his wife, Margene West Lloyd, the daughter of Jim and Alice West. The call was about their son, a student at the University of Utah, who had been struck by a car while riding his bicycle.

The driver was one of his fraternity brothers, a small irony in the kind of accident you hear about every day—except that young Lloyd was paralyzed. He had been transferred home to the Texas Institute of Research and Rehabilitation, age eighteen or nineteen, bed-ridden with a broken spine.

His parents did not call to discuss a lawsuit or money. They asked if I would stop by and talk to him. He blamed himself for the accident. The doctors had dealt with this problem often. If they couldn't get him out of his funk, his condition would grow more helpless.

We visited twice, and he had been reluctant to see me. The second time I did something I set out to do—make him angry. "What the hell was your crime?" I snapped at him. "All you did was ride your bicycle." His fraternity brother had run a red light.

He asked me to come back, and he seemed to look forward to our talks. I did not treat him as an invalid. That would have gained us nothing. I spoke to him as if something good was waiting to happen. Then, on his own, he decided he wanted to sue the driver of the car that hit him.

The doctors viewed this as the first encouraging sign they had seen—depression had made the turn to anger. We filed the suit in Utah, and it resulted in a very large settlement for the times. He became a friend of my sons and comes to my home every Christmas. He has adjusted beautifully to his circumstances. His is a life mostly of the mind, but he lives it fully.

Now we fast-forward a few years. Alice Sneed West, the daughter of a pioneer Texas settler, died in February of 1978. She left behind a will leaving nearly all of her estate to the three lawyers, who had brainwashed her. The Lloyds were being represented by one of the city's largest law firms. The lawyer at the firm handling the case called me and asked me to meet with the family. I was then asked to take over the case, in contesting the fraudulent will.

I am obligated to say that these lawyers denied every allegation of conspiring to enrich themselves at the expense of her natural heirs. I also feel obligated to say that there are attorneys who are corrupt, whose absence of ethics can never be ignored, and whose conduct is despicable.

One acted as the executor of her estate and the other as his substitute. Under the will, and a codicil to the will, they would have received most of her money and property. Her daughter, Margene, was left $100. Her granddaughter, Lillian Ferrell, was left $7,000, a painting, and one piece of jewelry. Nine other grandchildren were given $100 apiece.

The ultimate destination of every hog is the slaughterhouse.

Alice Sneed West was simply a victim, three deep in greed and bad intentions. They might as well have tied her up and left her on the railroad tracks. They used armed guards to control her and keep away her relatives. She was persuaded at one point to sue her daughter. Then they told her she had no daughters (one, Marian West Blakemore, had died). When the widow needed to be hospitalized, one of the lawyers took an adjoining room to make sure she had no visitors. Her head was filled with lies and booze and legal hash, until the palace guard coerced her to sign a will that she was mentally unable to fathom.

My temperament would have been best served by letting a judge and a jury decide if these lawyers had behaved properly, and to whom the estate properly belonged. But they quit. They gave up. The trio renounced any claims to the estate and waived any right to serve as executors.

My clients, the daughter Margene Lloyd, granddaughter Lillian Ferrell, and other grandchildren, received the bulk of the estate. The property consisted of $30 million in cash, the mansion, the ranch, an art collection that included a Gainesborough, antiques, and a safe with fine jewelry. There were other bequests to charity, to her church, and to former employees of Mrs. West.

Alice and Silver Dollar Jim West lived a Texas fairy tale. It was a pleasant duty to be able to give them a reasonably happy ending. I only regret that the men who tried to cheat their heirs went unpunished. On the other hand, they went away disappointed, like a vulture that bites into a glass eye.

Money being their goal, perhaps they were punished, after all.

THE SURVIVORS

The list of truly terrifying experiences, the kind that will guarantee that you wake up in the middle of the night, screaming, isn't long: an encounter with a great white shark. Being trapped on a submarine that sinks to the bottom of the sea. Falling into a giant blender at the Howard Johnson plant in New Jersey and being voted worst flavor of the month.

But the one most people share is a plane crashing into a mountain, in the winter, in a blizzard—no food, no help, no way to stay warm, the plane all but buried in the snow.

We have read the books and seen the movies and marveled at the incredible will to survive that the fortunate few exhibit. You think of a soccer team lost in the Andes,

In September of 1977, the surviving children were awarded a judgment of $14 million, at the time the highest personal injury settlement on record. Judge Shearn Smith signed the order, which provided monthly payments to the kids for the rest of their lives.

It is hard for me to realize that twenty-five years have passed since the case was closed and Andy and Mark Godfrey are pushing forty. In the law, we hear certain words so often they seem like catch phrases. "Pain and suffering" are even used to describe divorce actions. But there are cases that do remind us, as reluctant as we may be to think of them, what the words really mean.

AN EYE FOR AN EYE

Bob Aspromonte managed to play big league baseball for thirteen years without a disabling injury. Then, in 1976, five years after he had retired, he almost lost an eye trying to jump-start a car battery.

Bob was trying to drive away from a friend's office in Houston, where he had played third base his first seven seasons in the majors and now lived. When his car wouldn't start, the friend offered to assist him and positioned his own car with the engine running.

Aspromonte had attached a cable to one of the caps at the top of the battery and was leaning over the fender of his car, looking inside the hood to hook up the other clamp, when a cap flew off the battery and struck him in one eye. The pain was intense. The vision in that eye was gone.

He came to me for help. After a lengthy interview, I learned that he had purchased the cable from a Sears Roebuck store and the battery was standard equipment when he bought a General Motors car. Further, there was no warning on the battery or the cable.

I agreed to represent him. I filed the suit and developed the case, and General Motors quickly settled. That left Sears. I based our claim on a defect in failing to properly warn the user. The Sears attorneys wanted a trial, so I accommodated them.

Aspromonte faced multiple surgeries, and whether he would regain the sight in the injured eye was uncertain. The eye was discolored, gray, and unfocused. Lawsuits are not beauty contests, but as an athlete and a person Bob Aspromonte had been a young man with no flaws.

He had signed his first professional contract with his hometown team, the Brooklyn Dodgers, and wound up in Texas in an expansion draft. He was Houston's opening-day third baseman in 1962. He started there every year through 1968, rarely missing a game and delivering big hits on teams that did not win often enough to enjoy them.

He had the first hit and the first run by a Houston player, and he became an instant favorite with the fans. At least half the crowd fell in love with him. He was twenty-three and never could shake the image of the handsome bachelor and Italian matinee idol. (Some of us might question why anyone would want to shake it.)

When Bob traveled around the state with the team's first ticket caravan, a nightly ritual was getting him back on the bus before the wife of the most important man in town followed him home.

He still holds the franchised record for grand-slam homers in a career, six, two of them for a twelve-year-old from Arkansas, named Bill Bradley, who had temporarily lost his vision. The youngster came to Houston for an operation that was successful, saw Bob hit the second grand slam, and later became an eye surgeon. All of which sounds like one of those stories you might have read on the back of a Wheaties box.

Now here was Bob Aspromonte, half blind and emotionally scarred. I had sued Sears on his behalf for $875,000 and we tried the case in 1978. While the jurors were out deliberating, they sent a note with a question for

Judge Wallace. The question was, "Judge, do we have to give the amount Mr. Jamail asked for, or can we give him more money?" Judge Wallace instructed them that he could not answer and for them to follow the evidence.

The jury returned with a verdict for the full amount of $875,000. The Sears executives and their lawyers were outraged, swearing to the press that they would appeal and have this horrible miscarriage of justice overturned. Then something went awry for them. They let the time for filing an appeal pass.

I then made a move to collect the judgment. I prepared the proper legal documents, got a deputy sheriff to accompany me, and drove to the largest Sears store in Houston, at Main and Richmond Streets. It was noon, the Friday before Memorial Day, a big sales day.

The deputy and I walked into the store and went upstairs to the store manager's office. He was startled and asked what we wanted. I said that we wanted the keys to the store and ordered him to get on the loudspeaker system and tell the customers to leave, as we were closing the doors.

He thought I was a terrorist. I showed him the court order and told him that until the $875,000, plus interest, was paid, Bob Aspromonte and I owned the store. He looked as though he might have a stroke. He asked me what was going to happen. I said, "I'll tell you what is about to happen. Your competitor, Montgomery Ward, is about to have the biggest Memorial Day sale in history."

He was trapped. He asked if he could make a phone call. I said, sure, one call. He began to dial. He said he was calling the president of Sears in Chicago. I said, "That's not who I would call." He quickly hung up and asked who I would call. I said, "The lawyer in the firm that screwed this up." I gave him the lawyer's name, and within thirty minutes he showed up with his firm's check in the full amount.

The next day, the newspapers, radio and television stations all over town blared out the news: "Jamail Closes Sears." I received a lot of phone calls, many congratulatory, some curious, but the most interesting was from my pal Willie Nelson. All he said was, "Joe, you son of a bitch, don't you know it's un-American to shut down Sears?" And he hung up.

Over a period of years, and several operations, Bob Aspromonte regained nearly the full use of his injured eye. I was glad for Bob, who had class when a lot of athletes didn't have the time. He looked and behaved like a big leaguer. He was never loud or crude and rarely had a hair out of place. He and his two older brothers landed a Coors beer distributorship and became wealthy.

A good thing happened to good people.

A BUMPY RIDE

On Thanksgiving weekend of 1984, a sixteen-year-old Houston girl named Sonya Renee Webster was invited by a schoolmate to spend a Saturday at his family's farm.

After lunch, she and William Lipsey, also sixteen, decided to do some horseback riding and hopped on the family's three-wheeled Honda all-terrain cycle (called an ATC) to ride out to the barn. Miss Webster rode on the back.

As the two drove slowly down a path toward the barn, Lipsey took a left turn, and the ATC, advertised as a "super-trike," flipped. Renee, as she preferred to be called, was thrown from the vehicle. The impact broke her neck, leaving her a quadriplegic. Though she could move one hand enough to operate a motorized wheelchair, she was virtually paralyzed from the neck down.

She had literally exchanged a ride on an all-terrain vehicle for a wheelchair with with a motor. For a lovely, healthy teenager, this was a wretched, tragic tradeoff.

As a result of the accident, Webster, once a high school

tennis star, now lives under round-the-clock supervision in her small apartment two blocks from her parents' home.

For five years before the accident, Honda had advertised its ATC as "part tractor, part tornado," a vehicle that could move along trails "faster than a horse and cheaper than a pickup." And the cycle had neither a speedometer nor an independent suspension system.

While the Honda dealer who sold the ATC testified that it came with a sticker that warned against multiple riders, the Lipseys insisted they had not seen such a warning.

The parents of Renee Webster contacted me. As I reviewed the case it did not take long for my sense of outrage to start boiling. The three-wheeler was so lacking in stability that it was inherently dangerous, and Honda's advertising campaign, with its emphasis on breathtaking daring and excitement, was an invitation to an Evel Knievel kind of death-defying fun.

Honda's implicit warranties as to the ATC's safety were flagrantly violated by the super-trike's design. Honda had, in fact, portrayed the ATC as a speedy toy that could be driven by any youth. The defense assertions that Lipsey had been operating the vehicle incorrectly only served to further impeach the untempered claims in their television commercials and magazine ads.

But nothing offended me more than attempts by the defense to suggest that Renee and William were just two more "drug-crazed" teens. That characterization also enraged the families and the jury.

I appealed to the jury's role as the conscience of the community, a force that could send a message to both Tokyo and Main Street America. "Honda comes to this country to turn a profit," I said, "and they do. But in return we expect them to make their product of such quality that it doesn't kill or maim our teenagers." The jury really picked up on that theme.

In effect, Honda would have thrown Renee on a

human scrap heap, but I urged the jury not to let "the wrongdoers set their own punishment." They responded by finding the company 95 percent liable and the Lipseys liable for the rest. The damages of $16,597,602 (sixteen million, five hundred ninety-seven thousand, six hundred and two dollars) represented Honda's first loss in over one hundred cases involving the super-trike.

The money would improve the comfort and quality of Sonya Webster's life, assure of her of the best in health care and therapy, and give her at least access to more activity. That was justice.

Vindication was when Honda, because of this case, was forced to take off the market every all-terrain three-wheel cycle in the country.

This is the exercise of law at its most fundamental level, the protection of the public interest. If there is a distinction I believe justifies my existence on earth, it is this: I am personally responsible for three national recalls—by Remington Arms, Honda, and Parlodel drugs. They can engrave that on my tombstone.

Don't Count Your Chickens

In the civil courts, lawyers are rarely asked to do detective work. For some, it is enough of a challenge just to perform as a lawyer. But every great once in a while, you have no choice. What a witness says is in conflict with the evidence. The circumstances seem to lead to only one conclusion.

But something is missing. The picture is wrong. You know it. You can feel it. If you dig deeply enough, and hard enough, you can recreate a scene and overcome the weakness of what at first looks like a nothing case.

In 1985, I tried a lawsuit on behalf of a man named Donald Eubanks against a division of the Hughes Tool Company. So far, nothing unusual.

But Eubanks had been paralyzed from the waist down in a one-car collision late on New Year's Eve on the old Liberty Highway. He was obviously drunk. The legal definition of driving under the influence, intoxication, is 1 on the scale. Eubanks had tested at 2.8, over twice the legal limit, two hours after the crash.

An open-and-shut case.

Here is a man who was obviously drunk, whose blood had been drawn by impartial people at a local hospital. But there were two eyewitnesses with a slightly different story to tell. One good Samaritan had left a business card in the injured man's shirt pocket while he lay unconscious in a yard.

Billie Sue Crane and her husband were in the business of making and selling cement chickens, which they displayed on their lawn. When Donald's car left the highway, he careened across their front yard and knocked off the heads of about twenty of those chickens.

Another witness, who had been driving behind him, testified that Eubanks was not exceeding the speed limit, was in the proper lane, and was not weaving. Suddenly, the headlights of a large truck appeared in his lane, coming from the opposite direction. He wheeled his car to the right. The vehicle hit a ditch and flipped over. He was thrown into the yard, unconscious, paralyzed.

This witness had not seen the name of the truck. Another witness, parked at an intersection about one hundred feet from the scene, had been watching near a streetlight. He saw the truck pass by and noticed a red and blue logo on the side, but couldn't read the name. Each of the witnesses, independent of one another, said the truck crossed over into the right lane and kept going, while my man went into the ditch. This was the story they repeated when we took their depositions. We were fortunate one of them had left a card in his shirt pocket. Eubanks' parents brought it to my office. We conducted a search of what trucks would have been in the area around that time on New Year's Eve, and who had the right logo. It came down to one company, with a red and blue logo on the side of the door, and that was Hughes Drilling Fluids, part of Hughes Tool.

So I sued them and we went to court. The other side spent two days putting on drunk experts, after I had already told the jury how drunk he was. One of their main witnesses was a professor the company brought down from the University of Pennsylvania. They put him on the stand and calculated how many drinks he must have consumed. They must have spent $25,000 on charts alone.

When the defense had finished its examination, I looked at the professor and said, "Being drunk, one can still stay on his side of the road, can't he?"

"Yes," he responded, with reluctance.

"The point is, you don't know if the defendant's truck got on the wrong side of the road and made Mr. Eubanks hit the ditch or not, do you?"

"No, I don't know that."

"And the lawyers didn't tell you that was what happened, did they?"

"Well, no."

I said, "If that happened, and Mr. Eubanks was driving within the speed limit and on his side of the road, and the oncoming truck veered into his lane suddenly, what would be, in your expert opinion, Mr. Eubanks' first reflective move?"

He said, almost sheepishly, "He would turn the wheel to the right."

"Turn to the right!" I exclaimed. "No kidding. And if Mr. Eubanks did this, would he be acting like a reasonably prudent person? That is the charge."

Answer: "Yes, that is the reaction he would get."

I had made him my witness. Now I wanted to return to the charts for a minute. I said, "Step down from the witness stand, would you please, and take that pointer with you. Show the jury on that chart where you are if you have about five Scotches, on what part of the drunk scale would he be."

Suspiciously he said, "How is that relevant?"

I said, "Just curious. I want the jury to know what state I'm in every night around seven, because that's what I have. And you can go back to Pennsylvania, professor."

The jury cracked up and awarded us every cent for which we had sued. There was the forerunner of another precedent in that case. I asked the jury to give the two sons of Donald Eubanks a half-million dollars each, even though they were uninvolved in the accident and unhurt. This was before the time that children could recover from a father's injury. The court took that money away, but the interest brought it up to $7 million.

The headless chickens had come home to roost. The result was not an entirely satisfying one, because no amount of money can fully compensate a party for a crippled future. But the suit had a degree of difficulty and served as a tune-up for a test soon to come.

I tried the case about three weeks before I represented Pennzoil against Texaco.

STANDING ORDERS

On the last day of December 1993, Clarissa Diane Trawick was admitted to Memorial Hospital in The Woodlands for the delivery of her child.

The drug Parlodel was prescribed and given to Clarissa after the birth for the purpose of drying her breast milk, as she was not going to breast feed her baby. This drug was manufactured and sold by Sandoz Pharmaceutical Company.

Before 1993, Sandoz had received complaints that their drug had caused strokes in some females. The drug was originally used in relieving fluid retention in male arthritic patients. It was approved by the Food and Drug Administration for that purpose. There were other pharmaceutical companies making a similar drug.

After receiving warnings and complaints, the FDA, in its inept, bureaucratic way, asked the companies to take the drug off the market and not have it used for de-lactation. The FDA *didn't* demand it. They asked the companies to comply voluntarily!

Every company other than Sandoz did so.

I was able to prove that the Sandoz marketing people then stepped up their pushing of this drug. They had the market all to themselves. It was like owning the only doughnut shop in town.

Sandoz had its sales representatives traveling around the country, visiting hospital personnel to get their staffs to help promote it. They went to doctors, as well, and convinced many to put the drug on what is called "standing orders." That is, if a woman said she did not intend to breast feed, the nurses just automatically gave her Parlodel.

With a clear field, the money rolled in, and Sandoz made no effort to warn anyone that the drug had been associated with strokes as a side effect.

Clarissa was an unknowing victim. She suffered a stroke so severe that she had to give up her baby to her in-laws. She could not care for herself, much less an infant.

I filed her lawsuit. Soon afterward, the drug was discontinued for this purpose and removed from the market. There were no more "standing orders." I couldn't make Clarrissa well, but I could see to it that she was taken care of for the rest of her life.

The day the case was called to trial, we settled it for millions of dollars. The full-time help that Clarissa can now afford to assist her also made it possible to keep her child with her.

Arsenic, but No Old Lace

Samuel was born on August 14, 1992, with a skull that did not close and with brain tissues growing out of the crown of his small head. His heart was missing the third ventricle. He was partially blind and deaf, and his body temperature swung wildly. Samuel did not cry, but whimpered in a rhythmical manner.

He died at the age of two months as a result of toxic substances released into the air and water of the area in which his family lived. In this case, the toxin was arsenic.

A large chemical company did this, and then responded as the truly callous and indifferent often do when their actions cause something terrible to happen. They ignored and then denied it, until the families around Bryan, Texas, began to notice how many of them had to bury their babies.

Samuel was one of more than a dozen whose families or estates I represented. Their stories meant far more to me than cases of law. They became intensely personal. Some of the children were more or less deformed. Some suffered more or less. A handful lived beyond a few months, and at least one girl to the age of fifteen, but the quality of their lives was zero. I felt the anguish of the parents.

This wasn't war. This was cruel neglect practiced upon our neighbors, by people who think contamination is part of the cost of doing business. If the problem is ignored long enough, if no one complains loudly enough, then no one is the wiser.

During the Reagan years, it developed that the government had thousands of old nerve gas bombs lying around. Any leakage could be a disaster. The government periodically sends a bunny rabbit into the storage area as a test. If the rabbit dies, the gas is leaking. Or maybe the bombs are pregnant.

And the powerful scorn the powerless for feeling helpless.

The first couple to contact me did so after a similar case had been lost in the Rio Grande Valley. They were unable to leave home, so on a clear day I got in my car and met them at a little café in Bryan. They were a young couple, absolutely distraught.

They told me their story and showed me some newspaper clippings about a plant owned by a company called Elf Atochem, which made a chemical that would defoliate cotton. A byproduct of this chemical was arsenic, and they were storing the arsenic in pits and attempting from time to time to cover it.

I felt for these people. If you don't get involved in these cases emotionally, you should be doing something more detached, like handing out the insurance forms in the emergency room. I didn't know what I could do for them at the time, but I make a lot of decisions by feel—and this one didn't feel right.

This couple organized the other families and came to my office to meet with them. I took their cases. It was a litany of horror. Some of the children were born with their brains exposed, others with spines deformed, with terrible spasms. Most suffered from upper spinal cervical defects. None could function.

I retained three experts, two from Texas A&M and one from the University of Texas Medical Branch in Galveston, who knew a great deal about chemicals. They were skeptical in the beginning, but after some serious research they brought back their findings, and we were able to put together a family tree–type chart.

The investigation turned up the fact that this plant had been cited several times by the Texas Health Department and the Texas Water Department. When it rained in Bryan, arsenic would overflow into a nearby creek where children played and swam. And part of the town's drinking water had been affected.

All of the children who were afflicted or had died were

born within a half-mile radius of this plant. All the children were close to the same age, with a few exceptions. I learned from the medical literature we were able to uncover that there is a brief time during pregnancy, lasting from three to four weeks, when exposure to an arsenic-type chemical can prevent the cranium from being fully formed, causing all these problems.

We were able to determine with certainty through medical and chemical testimony that this was the case. I filed the lawsuit against Atochem and five other entities, including four officers or agents of the company. In legal circles, in the beginning, the suit was sort of laughed at, which fed my anger even more.

Then I took the first deposition—of the plant manager. I proved through his silence that it was a wrongful operation. I had issued a subpoena for his appearance and records. He didn't bring any. To my surprise, he brought with him a criminal lawyer I knew. At the outset, I warned him that any lying would be subject to the penalties for perjury. I could see I was dealing with a very nervous individual.

For about an hour and a half, he chinned himself on the Fifth Amendment. I kept asking the questions. What I was developing, and could prove, was that they had an informant in the state health department. He would warn them, a day ahead of time, when the inspectors were coming. And they would clean up the plant.

A grand jury investigation had started, or would shortly. After that one deposition, Elf Atochem wanted to talk. I was invited to New York to meet with the president of the company, the man in charge of their U.S. operation, and their New York lawyers and experts. Atochem was a subsidiary of Aquitaine, a French company.

I decided, "Okay, Joe, this is a chance to see what their experts are going to say." I took with me two of the paralegals, who were working on the case, and my three experts. We all trooped into these big, beautiful offices, and their lawyers proceeded to tell me, with diagrams, how none of this could have happened.

A couple of lawyers from Vinson & Elkins were also defending the case, and they were in the room. I could see them shaking their heads. They were telling the president of the company, a South African named Bernard Adjulay, not to go "one on one with Joe—and *don't* let him have a shot at your experts."

But Adjulay was smarter than his lawyers, so he let me cross-examine the experts without a deposition. By the time we finished, I had fairly well demolished each of their arguments. A high point for me was when one of them made the point that arsenic is present (in microscopic traces) in many products, including celery, which people eat routinely.

I said, "I never had chemistry, sir, but I have been told that there is a difference between organic arsenic and inorganic arsenic. But I would love for you to plead that. Come to court and argue that everybody who eats celery, who is going to have a child, will have one born with his brains outside his head."

(My experts would give me quick handwritten notes on how to exploit all they had argued and disclosed.)

As we were leaving, Mr. Adjulay said he would like to have dinner with me that night. I asked him if there would be anything to drink there. I knew what he had in mind. He would get this Texas hick drunk and I would sell out my clients.

We went to a fancy restaurant with a private room upstairs, the whole treatment. A few tables away, I saw one of my friends from Vinson & Elkins. I winked at him and he just shook his head.

My host started off by telling me that the company was just an affiliate of Elf Aquitaine, which had no responsibility, and that Atochem had limited assets and an insurance limit of $25 million.

I said, "That's just unfortunate. How difficult is it to change the name of a company in France?"

"What do you mean?" he snapped.

I said, "Well, it's going to be Jamail Aquitaine after we get through, Bernard. This isn't going to work."

He was a humorless man, and I could tell he was frightened. I said, "I'm going to give you one number, and then I'm going to finish my drink and leave. I have friends I want to drink with." I gave him a figure in excess of $100 million. And I would raise it as we discovered more damaging information.

He sputtered and said, "We could never agree to that."

I said, "Fine. That's one reason they built that red granite building in Houston. It's called a courthouse, and I'm looking forward to spending some time with you there. Maybe we can become friends."

I couldn't get out of my hotel suite the next morning. I was sitting there with an Olympic-style hangover and trying to suck down orange juice when I heard the pounding on my door. I invited Adjulay right in.

He got right to the point. Would I consider $60 million?

"I'll think about it," I said, "but not for very long. Matter of fact, I just did, and the answer is no."

He insisted again that they could not afford the figure I gave him.

I said, "You have to try very, very hard, Mr. Adjulay, because a jury is going to bankrupt you and I'm going to take every dime I can from you and give it to these children and their families. Now, are we clear?"

Back in Houston, I sent out a sweeping notice for a bunch of depositions and records. The next time I picked up my phone, I was told that the president of Atochem was in town with his New York lawyer and they wanted to see me.

When they walked into my office, I did not acknowledge the lawyer, a fairly strident man from one of New York's largest firms. After my guest made a few general remarks, I said, "Look, it's futile. As long as this man"—I motioned to his lawyer—"is sitting here as an obstructionist, we are not going to get anywhere. What I suggest to you, write down what you want to do, and when you finish write at the bottom, 'No!' and sign my name to it. Now you have to leave."

I wasn't trying to be rude—well, perhaps a little—but they had come to town hoping to kill me with kindness and steal a discount on the suffering of my clients. They had been in Houston four or five days when I heard from a lawyer at Vinson & Elkins I respected. I knew we could talk.

He said, "I know where you're coming from, but you have to come off that $175 million figure." The amount had risen as I added on penalties.

I said, "I'm prepared to do that."

We agreed on a figure, which the company could not pay in full. I placed all the children's money in trust, in annuities so they could be guaranteed care for the rest of their lives. I deferred my fee for nine years. The last payment arrived on Friday, December 4, 2002.

I had dealt before with this kind of adversary. First they are going to charm you, then outsmart you. I had asked Adjulay, "Do I look like I rode in here on the back end of a load of cantaloupes? Now settle down, Bernard." He was a restless, excitable sort.

We did not become friends, but I believed I did calm him down. The company later found a less dangerous way to defoliate cotton.

DEATH BY INDIFFERENCE

For most of my career, I have waged a running battle with the medical profession, and I suppose it will never really end. Once, I was asked to debate the director of the Harris County Medical Association. He had a core meltdown on the stage, and when he finished the moderator said, "Mr. Jamail, you have two minutes to respond."

I turned to the moderator and I said, "You may remind this doctor that when his predecessors were treating George Washington with leeches, the better to bleed him, mine were writing the Declaration of Independence and the Constitution."

Today my fundamental quarrel is with a medical profession dominated by insurance companies, who would limit the right to sue and to cap the damages of patients who suffer pain, injuries, and even death due to incompetence and neglect.

A case in point:

In November of 1987, after two years in a coma, Maria Irma Palacios, a Hispanic housewife, died at the age of thirty-nine, leaving four children without a mother. She had been admitted to the Medical Arts Hospital in Houston for a partial hysterectomy.

After the operation, still drowsy from the effects of general anesthesia, Maria complained of being cold. Minutes later, she lapsed into a coma that was the result of an astonishing series of botched procedures. She never regained consciousness.

The attending physicians removed her surgical tubes too soon after the operation. The three-hundred-pound woman was then left lying on her back—in spite of the basic dictates of positioning for obese patients after surgery. Nurses responded to her complaints of being cold by tossing a blanket over her and leaving her where she lay.

Mrs. Palacios, in acute respiratory distress, was falling prey to a severe lack of oxygen in the bloodstream. But her sensation of cold, as well as her low blood pressure, bluish pallor, and dilated pupils—all textbook symptoms of oxygen deficiency—failed to alert anyone to her condition.

To make matters worse, the recovery room nurse was not on hand. She had stepped out to attend a staff meeting, leaving in her stead a scrub nurse with no training in recovery room care. Mrs. Palacios—who was herself a trained nurse—was left in the hands of someone who had little idea of how to recognize post-operative danger signals.

All I needed was to meet Maria's four little girls to take the case, and if that sounds syrupy, I can only confess that I am a sucker for little girls.

An investigation revealed that the attending physician responsible for the mother's anesthesia had a pronounced history of alcohol and drug abuse. And he was not secretive about it. On his original application to Medical Arts Hospital, he had specifically included the fact that he had been fired from his last post because of drug abuse.

The testimony showed that he had been hired not only without any assurance that he had been rehabilitated, but that the hospital made no attempt to monitor his access to prescription drugs. He had worked less than five feet from a closet full of drugs and hadn't even been bound by ordinary hospital rules that place only nurses in charge of administering prescriptions.

He, at least, was remorseful. I felt his share of the blame was no greater than the failure of the managers of the hospital, who were, in fact, accountants in Cleveland, in it purely for the profit—people who didn't fret at all about proper health care. They hired submarginal doctors who would work cheap and took no steps at all to protect their patients.

As a result, the hospital fell into the hands of such an inattentive and incompetent staff that it came to resemble a halfway house. Even the chief of staff—who put the attending physician on the job—had a long history of alcoholism.

I told the jury: "Here you have a doctor who's honest enough to tell them flat-out that he's got a drug problem—and what do they do? They don't help him. They just say, 'Get in there and gas up those patients,' without regard to the consequences."

The jury was also clearly moved by the accounts of the gradual demise of Maria Palacios. Her decline was so complete that after a few months none of her four young daughters could bring themselves to visit her again.

In the wake of the tragedy, the doctor gave up his medical license. The Medical Arts Hospital was demolished two years after the botched procedures—about the time Maria Palacios was officially determined to be brain dead.

On November 18, 1987, the jury returned a verdict of $52 million in actual damages, including an astounding $26 million for her pain and suffering during her slow descent into death. It was, I was told, a record verdict.

REAL THREAT, MOCK TRIAL

A writer described the scene as a "bizarre brew of the real and the unreal, and sometimes it was hard to tell which was which."

I believe I can comfortably accept that description, although as a personal matter I had no problem whatsoever knowing the difference.

I had taken it as a high compliment when the American Bar Association asked me to act as the prosecutor in a mock trial of G. Gordon Liddy, the onetime FBI agent, convicted Watergate felon, and conservative talk show host.

Liddy had agreed to be the defendant in the mock trial, in on the hypothetical crime of inciting a radio listener to shoot a federal agent in the groin. Actually, the remarks were real. I can't say that Liddy was flattered to be invited to defend himself, but the evidence I go by is the fact that he was there.

The backdrop for the trial was the ballroom of the Marriott Hotel in downtown Chicago, in April of 1997.

Liddy took the witness stand for two hours and testified in a more open way than he had during the Watergate conspiracy trials in 1973. "Is burglary all right?" I asked him.

"It depends on what you burglarize," he replied.

Liddy, who had been disbarred as an attorney after serving a term in prison, added that "Stealing money because you are broke is one of the reasons I would consider to be invalid. But stealing information is okay." As to the millions of listeners who have made his syndicated radio show a conservative favorite, Liddy acknowledged that some of them were, in my phrase, "loonies. Yeah, looney tunes."

In truth, it was a fairly invigorating few hours, having a clash of egos with the wiry, bullet-headed former Nixon loyalist and operative. He did not disappoint me when he walked to the witness stand with a haughty demeanor and a posture as starched as his buttoned-down white shirt.

He was defended by Stephen G. Morrison, a corporate lawyer from South Carolina, who tried to keep the focus on his service in the FBI and as a prosecutor.

I thought it was more revealing when I pressed Liddy into admitting that he once told a caller named Gwendolyn that he, Liddy, "smelled of sperm and gunpowder."

In truth, it seemed that the scent the audience was picking up was a touch of fear. Liddy is a tense man, justifiably, although I do give him credit for a somewhat twisted sense of humor. When I finished with him, I thought he looked slightly wilted.

His face was a mask in search of an expression—a hard man to read. But G. Gordon said, in his deadpan manner, "If accurately reported in the press, this might prove illuminating to the general public on First Amendment issues." Some might consider it paradoxical to have Liddy offering constitutional lessons to the members of the bar.

In years past, the ABA, the largest organization of lawyers in the world, staged mock trials that rewrote history, as was the case in the early 1990s when a mock jury found Ethel and Julius Rosenberg not guilty of being Soviet spies. But never before had the make-believe zeroed in on a real, live defendant using allegations that were based, at least in part, on reality.

Liddy had indeed instructed listeners that in certain circumstances they should shoot federal agents in the head, if they are good marksmen, saying, "If you're not a real good shot, lower your aim—go for the groin."

Taking Liddy's real words, the ABA added this hypothetical situation: An avid Liddy fan seriously wounds a federal agent during a middle-of-the-night raid on the listener's home. Liddy, in the hypothetical, is charged under an aiding-and-abetting statute with encouraging the listener through his show to commit assault. (The case was based on an actual conversation that Liddy had with a caller on his syndicated show.)

In Liddy's defense, Morrison argued that the First Amendment protected "reasonable political speech, and no one should be jailed for that." Morrison called on the jurors, all lawyers, to stand by the Constitution. "If we cannot have freedom of expression for those that we despise, we don't believe in it at all."

I could not disagree more strongly. As the Supreme Court has ruled more than once, you can't shout "Fire!" in a crowded theater, and inciting an individual to violence is a classic example of speech not covered by the First Amendment.

In my summation, I noted that "Liddy agrees that he has a listening audience which consists of some real cuckoos, people who are just looking for a little encouragement to vent their frustrations. Liddy provided that encouragement with his inflammatory words and should not be allowed to hide behind the First Amendment. He is essentially saying, 'Hey, look, I can light the bomb as long as I got a big, long fuse and I'm not around when it happens.'"

In the end, the mock jury was not permitted to render a mock verdict. Thomas S. Brown, a Philadelphia lawyer who was the program chairman, said he and others were concerned over implications should actual charges ever be brought against Liddy. Somehow, I thought this concern seemed to validate my position.

Others, too, found the facts more disturbing than fiction. Richard Harris, of Massachusetts, said far too much of the day's subject matter was real: "The radio broadcast is real; the past history is real; the attitude is real. I would have advised Liddy not to show up."

THE NUMBERS GAME

Of all the white-collar crimes, accounting fraud is among the most vile because it steals not only assets, but hope and trust, the currency working people can least afford to lose.

In 1992, I tried such a case in Galveston on behalf of the United States National Bank against Coopers & Lybrand and a company called MiniScribe. This was a preview of the widespread greed and corruption that a decade later would cause a near panic from Wall Street to Main Street.

MiniScribe was a hot-shot computer hardware company touted by all the analysts, just like some of the high-flying dot-coms of the Internet era. In 1987, like Dudley Do-Right racing to save Little Nell from the railroad tracks, here came their auditors, Coopers & Lybrand, to prep them for an initial public offering to sell bonds.

The company had to obtain approval from the Securities Exchange Commission. For that they needed certain affidavits and documents, and the partner in charge would not sign off on them because the accounting procedures were irregular.

So Coopers & Lybrand removed him and brought in a

new partner, who signed off on the paperwork the next day. Then they sold the bonds—a piece of cake.

What the evidence later revealed was a scheme as artfully simple as any bait-and-switch con job. These computer disks were about the same shape, size, and weight of a house brick. The company would bundle them up and send them to their retailers as inventory going out and accounts receivable. Next they would send out their agents to intercept them before the customers could get possession, then put them back in stock.

It was easier than stealing candy from a baby, because babies will cry.

I filed a lawsuit on behalf of the United States National Bank and the people who were hurt through their trust departments. There were Catholic and Episcopal churches, a synagogue, the schoolteachers' retirement fund. All of those people were burned because they had money in the trust fund at that bank.

We caught a break. A man who never would reveal his name called my office. He said to look at certain documents. They had not yet been produced, but a man with a conscience gave us a kind of road map. He would call and talk to one of our associates, Frank Staggs. Finally, Frank said, "Do you mind if I record this? I'm afraid I can't remember all of it." He agreed. We named him "Deep Throat."

Part of the accounts-due system was to spot check inventories. We soon were in a position to prove that they really did not. Late in 1989, after learning that MiniScribe was accused of fraud, Kempner Investments sold its bonds, taking a loss of $13 million, much of it the bank's trust department money.

We were in Denver, taking depositions, when a witness began shaking. I listened and turned to Frank, who looked at me and mouthed the name of our anonymous source, our very own Deep Throat.

When we went to trial, we had calculated a $12 million loss in actual damages. The defendant, Coopers & Lybrand, had maybe twenty-five lawyers lined up. Jimmy Lynn, the lead lawyer for the accounting firm, had told a few people he was going to Texas to kick my ass. Hey, I've seen *High Noon* a time or two. I love it when the Clantons ride into town.

The trial lasted three months, and halfway through I was doing some heavy damage. Frank Staggs was trying it with me, along with John McEldowney and Andy Mytelka, whose firm had referred the case to me for trial in Galveston. Everybody the other side brought out I was able to eviscerate, and I mean that in a nice, clinical way.

One day they came in as though the case were all over. They didn't unsnap the locks on their briefcases, much less unbuckle their gun holsters, and the jury was walking in. Jimmy Lynn handed me a formal letter, and I looked at it and saw that it was an offer for $20 million. I crumpled it into a tight ball, threw it down, and told him to make a suppository out of it. McEldowney was shaking like a leaf. "Are you crazy?" he said. "Are you crazy?"

At the recess, I said to the client, "You told me to use my judgment. Do you want me to take their offer?"

He said, "Whatever you say, Joe."

I said, "No, now listen to me. I will try this case forever. You tell me if you're a player or not."

He said, "Play."

I said, "Sit down right here, Mr. Kempner." This was Shrub Kempner, from an old Galveston family, whose management and investment firm was based on the island, once a favorite port of call for the pirate Jean LaFitte.

The jury went out and came back with a verdict for $568 million. That was before there was a cap on punitive damages. And they found fraud. That would have bankrupted Coopers & Lybrand, because any time an accounting firm is found guilty of fraud, the company is automatically stopped and enjoined from doing any SEC work. So they had to come to the table.

That was, to my knowledge, the first major conviction in the 1990s for accounting fraud. And they could not make it disappear by chanting, "Bookkeeping error." They had destroyed records.

My next one came along in the year 2000—also known as Y2K, when so many people were predicting all sorts of meltdowns. I was representing the United States National Bank again, versus Arthur Andersen. There is a confidentiality order attached to the settlement and I am unable to specify how much was paid, but it was millions and millions.

This was two years before the Enron catastrophe. Have they learned nothing? And to paraphrase the words of the courtly old Boston lawyer Joseph Welch, who took on the famous demagogue Senator Joe McCarthy, "Have they no shame?"

The case was just unsealed in the late spring of 2002. In the motion for a summary judgment, the engagement partner, Phil Harlow, told about the destruction of records. I took only one deposition. That was all I needed. Arthur Andersen had destroyed every record, electronic or written, that did not agree with their "final audit."

Chainsaw Al Dunlop had taken over Sunbeam, and that was how Arthur Andersen got involved. We sued both, but we separated the cases because we knew the company was going to file for bankruptcy.

Of course, it belabors the obvious to say that Arthur Andersen is no stranger to the destruction of records. They fired David Duncan, claiming he should not have done such a nefarious deed. Yet Phil Harlow still worked for them as of the late summer of 2002.

I asked him a question I suspect many investors would have enjoyed asking: "Do you store accounting data—that should be evidence—in trash barrels at Arthur Andersen?"

CHAPTER 3

PERCY

Percy Foreman was the last of a generation of lawyers who could claim a spiritual and physical link to the grandeur of Clarence Darrow and William Jennings Bryan.

I was never one for having heroes or role models, other than my father, but Percy came close. I was indebted to him. A year after I left the district attorney's staff, he began to refer clients to me, much to the chagrin of the larger plaintiff firms. The word got around: If Percy doesn't know where to send them, who does?

If you gained his respect, he demonstrated it with both phrases and action. On a local television show, my name came up for some obscure reason and he said, with no hesitation, "This country has never produced a better trial lawyer than Joe Jamail." This was in the late 1960s, and my biggest cases were still ahead of me. Percy had no need to flatter me. Yet he asked me to represent him on the two occasions when his own interests brought him to court. These were, of course, blessings of a mixed kind.

Once, he had raised a larger banner on the front of a building he officed in, declaring the space to be "THE TEMPORARY LAW OFFICES OF PERCY FOREMAN." This was some decades before advertising by lawyers was regarded as even somewhat acceptable, and the state bar association took a dim view of this behavior. A committee chaired by federal judge John Singleton was appointed to discipline Percy, twelve prominent lawyers who were going to teach a lesson to this grizzly of a man. As his attorney, I instructed him not to talk. After some debate, the committee decided to dismiss the matter if Percy would simply take down his sign.

Percy reacted as he usually did when people tried to tell him what he could or could not do. "Joseph, my boy," he said, "if that banner offends these honorable gentlemen on this committee, you can assure them, you can promise them, that with these bare hands I will rip it from its moorings and replace it with a banner twice as large that says, 'THIS IS NOT THE TEMPORARY LAW OFFICES OF PERCY FOREMAN."

He once handed me another message for the committee that I refused to submit. This is part of that message:

> At one time, my last will and testament provided for the setting aside of certain industrial businesses with a present cash market value of up to Two Million Dollars ($2,000,000) for the establishment of psychological research for a test in the evaluation of lawyers. The idea was to ascertain the relative merit of individual members of the Bar. There were several rationalizations for this Foundation. One would be to serve the lawyer himself. He would be permitted to know from a scientific analysis exactly how he rated in the legal

profession. That is, whether he was a .22 caliber, a .32 caliber, a .44 caliber, a .45 caliber, or a .357 Magnum—or just a .22 caliber in a .45 caliber frame.

The second point in the thinking behind this classification was that after a proper evaluation, he could paint on his letterhead, business cards, and door his proper scientific classification and charge fees accordingly.

Lastly, it was considered that eventually medical research might furnish a basis for the equalization of all attorneys. This would, of course, call for tranquilizers to be administered to the more resourceful, imaginative, and hard-working attorneys so as to slow them down to the norm. But mainly it was thought that some of the newer mental drugs might be mixed with pep pills and put cockleburs under lawyers who sat on their dead asses and expected their licenses to support them.

There it is. I felt I owed him a few last words from the grave, and the bar can take whatever action seems appropriate. He always said he would see his critics in hell.

Percy was one of the legendary criminal attorneys of his day, and over the years four hundred of his clients, accused of murder most foul, owed their freedom or survival to him. Still, he was always plotting bigger things until, sadly, time passed him by. He represented James Earl Ray, the assassin of Martin Luther King, just long enough to persuade Ray to sign a confession in a move to save Ray's life. Almost on his death bed, Percy was contemplating a white paper on Lee Harvey Oswald that would, he believed, make him "a giant figure in the history of criminal justice."

To many of us, he already was.

A large, shambling man with unruly brown hair

streaked with gray, one lock of which invariably fell over his forehead, Foreman could shrink a room by walking into it. He was the son of the sheriff of Polk County, a boy who grew up sleeping on the ground floor of his father's jail, a youngster who at the age of eight saw a man hanged. He remembered it as a public holiday, the farmers coming into town on wagons and the kids selling souvenirs and cotton candy.

Both his grandfathers fought with Hood's Brigade in the Civil War. He owed his beaked nose and opaque brown eyes, he said, to one of his mother's Cherokee ancestors.

Before he was fifteen, Foreman left home and moved to Houston, seeking brighter lights and better times. He took a job as a stenographer for a Texas oil company, and on the side he worked out at the YMCA with visiting wrestlers, among them Cyclone Mitchell and Strangler Lewis. By 1919, he said, he had developed so much technique on the typewriter that he finished second to Billy Rose at the national speed-typing contest in Atlantic City.

Through the 1920s, he studied law during the winters and spent his summers on the old Chautauqua circuits, traveling through the river towns in the Ohio Valley. Those high-flown tent shows would move into a town for three nights a week, featuring one-act plays and the great orators of the day. One lecturer was William Jennings Bryan.

At seventeen, Foreman started out as an advance man. "My towns were always full," he boasted, "people as far as the eye could see." Shortly he was promoted to platform manager, then to second day lecturer and, inevitably, to a featured role as a "last-night speaker." He learned to talk for marathon lengths of time on such topics as "The High Mission of Women in the Twentieth Century," "The American Social Ideal," and "The Canary Bird in the Coal Mine."

Eventually admitted to the bar in Houston, he set himself up in practice by distributing fancy printed cards that read, "Moses, Justinian, Blackstone, Webster and Foreman." Usually, he conducted his defense on the premise that Texas lawmen compared in sensitivity to the Gestapo.

"You want to know how it works in Texas?" he once said. "I'll tell you. The cops arrest the last person to see the deceased alive or the guy who finds the body. Then they beat him until he confesses."

He sat briefly on the state's side as a tough assistant district attorney—"I was Saul before I was Paul," he explained. He became known as "the Smoking Gun Lawyer." In Texas, it became an article of faith that people standing next to a body with a smoking gun in their hand demanded to consult with Percy Foreman.

His reputation grew to the point that a state legislator, arguing for the abolishment of capital punishment, declared that "Nobody who has the money to hire Percy Foreman has any real fear of the death penalty."

His clients saw it the same way. A rich Texan charged with homicide once said that he could not decide whether to hire Foreman and spend the rest of his life in poverty, or gamble on a moderate prison sentence and keep his estate.

As a lawman's son, Foreman offered quite a contradiction. A Houston sheriff and a Texas Ranger once gave him a beating in a courthouse hallway after he won a murder acquittal. A month earlier, two hundred Texas peace officers had presented him with a diamond-studded watch after his successful defense, without a fee, of four cops accused of brutality.

His moods, out of the courtroom as well as inside, were volatile.

This was the legendary lawyer I had to represent in a classic sore back case. He had sustained a neck injury in a traffic accident when his car was rear-ended by some-one driving a truck for Blue Bonnet Express. It was the type of case, and certainly Percy was the type of client, that a judge or jury might view with reservations. I don't think there was another lawyer in town who would have touched it.

For two reasons I needed a sophisticated jury. One, so much had been written and repeated about Percy. Two, he had suffered no loss of income during his recovery from the accident. In fact, he was making more money because the pain kept him awake at night, so he stayed up and worked on his cases, he said.

The foreman of the jury turned out to be an engineer, a graduate of MIT, someone who was fairly high up in the hierarchy of one of the space companies at NASA. We caught a break there. We also drew Judge John Snell, one of the meanest judges in town but fair. If you really crossed him, he might not sit still for it. He might just step down from the bench and kick you out of his court-room.

Right off, before the voir dire, the other side made a motion to the judge to have Percy turn over to them his income tax returns. You couldn't get any damages if you couldn't show any losses. Percy told me to tell them to go screw themselves.

When Judge Snell asked, "Mr. Jamail, what does Mr. Foreman say?", I replied, "Judge, I can't repeat it. The IRS has been trying to get his records for twenty years, so I don't think this group is going to have much luck."

We were off to a shaky start. While I was questioning a young woman in the jury pool, she answered in a voice so soft and low that she was barely audible. Percy grabbed me by the back of my coat and almost pulled me down. He said, "Make her speak up. I can't hear her."

I really don't know what made me do what happened next. Percy was a famous name and face, the best-known criminal lawyer in the country. But something made me decide that either *I* was going to try this lawsuit or he would trample me. I turned to him and said in a loud voice, "Mr. Foreman, it isn't important if you hear her or not. The only thing important is that I hear her. Now, shut up."

Then Judge Snell jumped in. "You have a lawyer, Mr. Foreman. Now sit down and be quiet."

From that point on, Percy was a model child, right up to the moment they took him over on cross-examination. I had helped him climb into the witness stand, wearing a neck brace, wincing with pain, to establish that he had no history of any problems with his neck or back, with one exception. When he was a young man, he testified, a very large horse had fallen on him and injured his back. However, being young he had overcome the injury and had encountered no problems since that time.

The attorney for Blue Bonnet, Mr. Gay Brinson, of the venerable law firm of Vinson & Elkins, cocked his head and asked, "Did I hear you correctly? You never had a neck injury before?"

Percy nodded and said, "Yes, that's right. Never."

The attorney motioned to the back of the room and two of his associates pushed a steamer trunk down the aisle, the kind they carry on large ships. Damned, I could not believe my eyes. He began to fish hospital records out of that trunk, and there must have been two hundred pounds of documents in there. He entered into evidence the records that showed Percy Foreman had on nine occasions, prior to this latest accident, checked into one hospital or another across the country because of neck pain.

He was suing for a popped neck. He had denied on the stand having any previous problems. He had denied it in his deposition.

What to do? The jury was staring at me, and I could

sense what they were thinking. *Give us an answer, Joe, or we'll blow you away.* And I wanted one, as well. I was thinking, "If the big man has stuck me out here in front and hasn't given me all the facts, I'll just run it right at him." I went with my own spontaneous reaction.

I said, "Percy, suppose you tell this jury and me why you didn't mention all these hospital admissions?" I was almost screaming at him. You have seen a kid dig his toe in the dirt when he gets caught at something? That was how he looked. In a voice that reminded you of the old actor Wallace Beery, Foreman said, "Aw, Joe, don't get mad at me. I didn't think that was important."

Quickly, I softened. "Well, I don't either. The important thing is that you WERE hurt in this accident." And we just went from there. In my closing argument, I faced the jury and said, "This lapse can't be explained in a satisfactory way. But neither can the cruelty of the defense. Let me render to you some of the things Percy Foreman has done. He has stood for the poor and the innocent and made sure the system worked for all people. They are asking you to stamp the word 'Liar' on his professional tombstone, and I am asking you not to. He has been a truly great lawyer. Now he's an old man, over the hill, growing a little senile."

About this time a great roar went up, and it came from Percy. "You goddamned son of a bitch!" he shouted. The courtroom froze. I turned to the jury and shrugged and said, "See what I mean? He doesn't even know where he is."

The jurors filed out, and when they returned, for some strange reason, they gave us four dollars more than we had sought—seventy-five thousand and four dollars. The judge took away the four bucks, but Percy collected every penny of the rest of it. Well—Percy and me.

I have been described as "flamboyant" myself a time or two, but when you are talking about Percy Foreman you are using an entirely different scale. If his clients lacked cash, he cheerfully accepted anything else of value—boats, cattle, fiddles, limousines, washing machines. He always said, only half-joking, that if he won the acquittal of a client who was guilty, the payment of his fee assured that they would not go unpunished.

About the only thing Percy had no interest in was ever being a judge. His reasoning was simple. "A judge has to see two sides, and there is really only one side in a lawsuit. My side. I'm an advocate."

So he was, and, in his time, the best criminal lawyer of them all.

CHAPTER 4

THE ESTATE

This is the story of a family feud, of immense wealth and power and greed, all the elements of a dynasty-type motion picture. Which is appropriate, in a way, because the intrigue that underpins the story had its beginning in Hollywood in 1932.

In that year, Lillie Cranz Cullen, traveling with her parents, met a man named Paolo di Portanova, was swept off her feet, and fell in love. He claimed to be an actor, although he was driving a taxi at the time. He also claimed to be a baron, a title he had traced back to 1740, although none of the standard reference works on European nobility supported his story.

Lillie was the eldest of four daughters of Hugh Roy Cullen, the oilman whose philanthropy helped established Houston as a world-class city. Lillie married Paolo, a short, suave man with a pencil-thin mustache, moved to California, lived for a time in Italy, and gave birth to two sons, Enrico and Ugo. Ugo was described as mentally troubled.

How the Cullens felt about their daughter's union was never a part of the public record, but she was estranged from the family for the rest of her life.

When Mr. Cullen died in 1957, he left behind nine hundred leases on some of the richest oil fields in Texas and Louisiana. The family holdings would grow to include a refinery on the Gulf Coast, oil exploration ventures in the Arab Emirates and the North Sea, a bank holding company, and real estate properties that included four square blocks of downtown Houston.

By 1961, Enrico di Portanova, who preferred to be called "Baron," had filed the first of several lawsuits seeking a greater share of the family trust. That year, he moved from Rome to Houston to better pursue his claim. In 1966, his mother died in New York, where she had lived an eccentric life in a seedy hotel, dressing like a bag lady. A few months before her death, Enrico and his father had Ugo declared *non compos mentos* so they could become the guardians of his care and his share of the estate.

Lillie left an inheritance of $4.8 million to her two sons.

The three younger daughters had married men home from the war in 1945 and 1946, and the husbands quickly settled into their father-in-law's business empire. And in time the three men, joined by the children of H. R. Cullen's only son, Roy Gustav, who died young in an oil field explosion in 1936, grew to fill Mr. Cullen's role as pillars of Houston society.

The lawsuits had been festering for twenty-one years when I entered the case in 1982. I had received a call one day from Roy Cullen, a close and valued friend whose home was back to back with ours. The family and its company, Quintana, had been represented for many years by the highly efficient law firm of Vinson & Elkins.

Roy asked if I would take over as the lead attorney, and I hesitated. The assignment would be a difficult one, stepping into the thick of a case as drawn-out as this one, which had grown now to involve more than forty lawyers, accountants, and investigators. I asked him to arrange a meeting the next day with the rest of the family.

Corbin Robertson was there, as were Isaac Arnold, Harry Cullen, and Roy, with their wives. We talked for about ten minutes and I said, "Okay, I'll do it." They smiled and looked relieved, and Wilhemina Robertson asked, "What is your fee going to be?"

I looked at her and said, "Until you asked, it was going to be nothing." I paused. "It's still nothing, so don't ask again."

The case was a spider web of financial threads and so many players that the drama now had echoes of Rudyard Kipling: lawyers to the left of us, lawyers to the right of us, volleyed and thundered.

Part of my motivation was to disengage from this mess one of the city's first and finest families, people who were raised with a social conscience and a sensitivity to the community's needs. But as a professional incentive, it was enough to know that God had delivered to me Roy Cohn, the New York lawyer who headed the di Portanova posse and had been Senator Joe McCarthy's henchman in the heyday of the communist witch hunts. Cohn had been exposed in the Army–McCarthy hearings as an oily figure as ruthless and reckless as his boss, but he remained popular with political groups on the far right.

And I was elated to have the resources of Vinson & Elkins, who were so proficient and so generous. Ewing Werlein, now a federal judge, John Carter, and Gib Walton prepared the case files for me. It was like climbing a wall of paper. In their briefings, they cut to the core and got me to a point where I could focus on the issues.

We had to trust one another as professionals. It was not so different from bringing in a doctor for a second opinion. If one was too thin-skinned to adjust, one needed to find another line of work. This was a pitched battle, not a minuet.

The di Portanovas had filed a new suit in 1980, alleging that an earlier settlement in 1969 had not given them a fair share of the estate. The suit claimed that their mother had been excluded from the family partnership and therefore they were entitled to a percentage of every investment the family had made over the past twenty years.

In 1981, Enrico's income from the trust he inherited had been $1.3 million—per month. If their suit was successful, the amount owed could run into the hundreds of millions of dollars, maybe a billion.

The lawsuit was brought in the probate court of Harris County, Texas, Pat Gregory presiding. The opposing relatives had lawyers, the banks had lawyers, and the courts had added lawyers. The Cullens thought they were being battered by the rulings of the probate court, while Enrico's entourage was having a jolly time traveling all over the continent, holding meetings, talking to each other, billing it as court costs.

The first thing I did was call the judge and ask if I could come over and visit with him. I had known Pat Gregory a long time and had represented his son. I have found that if questions of ethics are in the air, there is no substitute for looking someone in the eye. "Judge, I need to know one thing," I said, and it was clear I had disagreed with some of his rulings. "Is it possible for my clients to get a fair trial here?"

He said, "Joe, are you getting in this case?"

I said, "I already am."

He said, "The answer is yes."

I went back to my office and a minor scandal soon

arose out of this meeting, as I guessed it would. Had I tried to pressure the judge?

I wanted oral arguments, not just rulings, and now the climate in the courtroom was changing. I raised questions about the dealings between the banks and the di Portanovas. When Enrico billed the trust, one bank would transfer the funds to another before cutting a check—5 percent going in and 5 percent going out, leaving blood all over the courtroom.

Every day brought a new sideshow. I took the deposition of the old man, Paolo, who spoke fluent English. Except that, suddenly, in the middle of the deposition, he misplaced the language and needed an Italian interpreter. There was not enough Lysol in the stores to erase the stink from this case.

I took the deposition of Enrico, who could remember nothing but insisted that I refer to him as "the Baron di Portanova." I said, "Sir, I couldn't do that. I'm an American citizen. But perhaps we could have a compromise."

He said, "What kind?"

I said, "Suppose I call you an asshole, or a poseur?"

I was able to get the judge to strike a couple of his prior rulings, and then another strange development took place. I asked him to set a date for the trial, I was ready to proceed, and now Roy Cohn and his local counsel, Babe Schwartz, were running around making charges against Pat Gregory. They filed a motion for recusal based on the fact that their own lawyers had done business with him and had loaned him money.

All of which I knew, and I had remained silent. Asked for a comment by the press, I said simply, "I'm aware of all these facts and all I care to say is I am ready for trial." The bastards had fallen out with each other, and the case was transferred to the court of Judge Bill Bear.

What other lawyers missed about me was this: What

they did for money, I did for pleasure. I enjoyed intimidating opposing lawyers to break their concentration. During one of the hearings, I stood up and walked near Roy Cohn while slowly observing: "What I see here is a strange, weird, queer . . ." I let the sentence hang in the air for a moment while Cohn's face turned red, then I finished with the word, ". . . motion."

Later, I pushed my way into one of his press conferences and said, "I've checked on Cohn, and he hasn't gone to trial in sixteen years. I figure I'm going to have to whip him with barbed wire to get him into court."

In May of 1984, Judge Bear granted us a summary judgment, ruling that the key questions of law involved in the case should be decided in favor of the Cullen heirs. The di Portanovas were owed nothing and were ordered to pay the costs.

I had argued that Quintana was an accounting mechanism and not an entity for doing family business. I had appealed to common sense, saying, "It is past time, long past time, that the court puts an end to this lawyer's relief and pension fund." Both arguments needed to be heard. But in the end, the judge ruled that the 1969 settlement barred any new claims by the di Portanovas.

They would lose on every appeal, and Roy Cohn stayed with the case until just before the bitter end. A lawyer with the New York firm of Arnold Porter showed up for a hearing in the Court of Appeals, running into a packed courtroom at the last minute, wearing an expensive suit and a backpack. He was representing the di Portanovas.

He walked over to the jury box, where Alvin Owsley, a partner at Baker Botts and a friend of mine since law school, was quietly sitting, and asked him which one was Jamail. Alvin looked at him and with a sly grin on his face poked his index finger in my direction.

I said, "Sir, do you always wear that backpack when you come to court?"

He said, "I just came in from the airport."

I said, "Sir, you're wearing that thing six inches too high if you're trying to protect the part of your anatomy I'm after."

Even Roy Cohn smiled at that. He finally knew he had been beaten. He wasn't gracious in defeat, and I didn't want him to be. I wanted him to be the kind of person he had been all his life, when he had hurt so many people so needlessly. He is dead now, but that changes nothing. Alive, he would be inconspicuous in a commode.

Enrico di Portanova continued to collect his $15 million a year and maintain his jet-set lifestyle, maintaining homes in Houston, New York, Acapulco, and Monte Carlo. He had divorced his first wife and married a lovely Houston girl, Sandra Hovas, whose family owned a chain of furniture stores. In the last lawsuit to be dismissed, the attorneys for Ugo di Portanova sued Ricky and Greg Hovas, Sandra's brother, for mismanaging Ugo's estate.

In an ending to their story that many found haunting and eerily romantic, both the baron and the baroness, as they preferred to be called, died of cancer within a few months in the year 2000.

The names of the Cullen family members are still rarely seen on the society pages. But the name appears all over town on boulevards, hospitals, office towers, and college campuses.

A final trivia note: When Judge Bill Bear dismissed the case, there were forty-five lawyers in his courtroom, in one capacity or another.

CHAPTER 5

READY! AIM! CLICK!

Most attorneys do not daydream about playing Perry Mason. They are happy to get through a day without misplacing their glasses or car keys.

It so happened that I did uncover a clue that solved and won a case. It only happened once, but if you work it right, once is enough.

If you believe that lawyers spend much of their time getting on or off the telephone, I can tell you that perception is on the money. And this case began with a call that took an unexpected turn.

I was working on a lawsuit on behalf of a young woman who had suffered brain damage in a car accident. The defendant was being represented by an Austin insurance attorney named John Coates. I had clashed with his firm on several occasions, and at least one of those times was what I tend to refer to as a bloodbath.

So there was no special fondness between us, and I

felt no distress when one of his partners called to say that Coates would not be defending the case. Then he told me why and made the kind of request I find hard to resist. To begin with, I believe in helping people if you can. And two, when a competitor asks for your help, you accept the request as the compliment it is.

In September of 1977, Coates was hunting with his son, Will, and two district court judges. Young Will had been in a deer blind waiting for a deer that never appeared. His rifle, a Remington Mohawk 600, which had been a present from his grandfather, was set on safety. At one point, he thought he spotted a deer and pressed down on the trigger.

Realizing that the safety was on, he moved it partway off, only to discover that the target had vanished. He then moved the safety to the "on" position and heard the horn of his father's car honk, telling him that the party was ready to leave.

Leaving the safety on, Will walked back to the car and climbed in, with one of the judges holding the door for him. His father was sitting in the front seat and, as Will got in, the elder Coates asked if the gun was loaded. Because the rifle was in fact loaded, and good gun-handling practice calls for weapons to be carried unloaded in vehicles, Will followed the usual procedure for unloading the rifle.

The Mohawk 600 is designed so that it cannot be unloaded with the safety in the "on" position. It must be switched to "off" first. Will pushed the safety to the "off" position as he sat in the back of the car, and as he did so the gun discharged, firing the bullet in the chamber into his father's back, through his spine, and into a kidney.

Will screamed, "My God, I've shot my father!"

The judges saved John Coates' life by getting him quickly to the nearest town, breaking into a locked hospital emergency room to use the telephone, and getting a medical evacuation helicopter to the scene. The bullet left Coates paralyzed from the tenth thoracic vertebra down, and minus a kidney, in addition to other internal damage. He lay near death for more than a month.

The accident also left his fourteen-year-old son paralyzed with grief and guilt over the fact that he was holding the weapon when it fired. He was convinced that he was responsible for his father's injuries. Initially, it seemed that the trial lawyer's career was at an end and that young Will would bear the scars of the disaster permanently. Most people who heard about the mishap assumed it happened because of faulty gun handling on the son's part.

I listened with genuine heartache to the story told me by John Coates' law partner Donald Thomas, who happened to be Lyndon Johnson's lawyer. But when he reached the point of asking for my help, it was not on behalf of the now paralyzed lawyer. The other partners, and friends and relatives of the Coates family, were terribly concerned about the mental state of Will Coates. The partner knew that I had established a reputation for being able to analyze accidents and find highly qualified experts to testify in complicated cases.

At that point, no one was thinking about a lawsuit— who would they sue? They were just hoping that I could locate a firearms expert who would examine the rifle and perhaps determine if there had a malfunction—a finding that would help ease the trauma of a fourteen-year-old boy.

I assured him I would do whatever I could. The partner brought the Mohawk 600 rifle to my office. I knew just the right man to consult as an expert—someone whose name I guard to this day. He had been a general in our U.S. Army. I reached him by phone and began to describe the accident to him. Halfway through the conversation, the expert told me to stop and said, "You don't have to say anything more. I know what happened, and the gun you are talking about is a Remington Mohawk 600, isn't it?"

I was flabbergasted. Immediately, all the adrenaline started flowing and I knew we were on to something. I delivered the gun to the expert, who lived in a small town outside of Houston. He explained to me that with a round in the chamber and pressure on the trigger, a later movement of the safety to the half-safety position would cause a small part called the *sear* to drop down slightly from its original position in the trigger housing, exposing the firing pin. Moving the safety back to the full safety position would not move the sear back up in certain guns, and any later movement of the safety into the "fire" position would cause the safety mechanism to act as a second trigger, firing the weapon in whatever direction it was pointed. All of this could happen at any time after the trigger had once been squeezed, even months after the user's memory of whether the gun was loaded had completely faded.

That analysis convinced me that, in addition to Will Coates being blameless, there probably was a strong products liability claim against the manufacturer, the Remington Arms Company, which was a subsidiary of the DuPont Company. Remington had employed a design that would not permit the user to unload the gun in the "safe" position (which would have eliminated the danger completely) and had allowed a number of the guns to get through quality control with the metal tolerances off enough for the sear to drop when the safety was used.

Avoiding or finding a remedy for either of these two defects would have produced a weapon that, while not foolproof, would have been forgiving of a momentary oversight that could be expected in normal use. Numerous other manufacturers had taken care to see that their products forgave minor deviations from prescribed procedures, so why not Remington? Perhaps they had known about the problem. I intended to find out.

First, though, there was young Will Coates to think about. After some further precision testing by mechanical engineers, I took the gun back to Austin for a meeting with two of John Coates' partners and with Mrs. Coates, but initially without Will. I demonstrated the defect as the expert had. Then I slipped a cartridge from which the powder had been removed into the chamber and called Will into the room.

The youngster hated to even see the gun again, much less handle it. But I prevailed on him to take it and demonstrate exactly what he had done. When he got to the "safety on" stage, the firing pin struck the back of the powderless cartridge and the muted report showed everyone present that, had a regular round been in the rifle, it would have fired again.

Will Coates was ecstatic with relief, and Mrs. Coates and the law partners were galvanized into action. They asked me to sue Remington on behalf of John Coates, who was still in intensive care, barely able to talk because of the tubes in his throat. The lawsuit was filed against Remington and the dealer who sold the gun, claiming $7 million in compensatory damages and an unspecified sum for punitive damages.

My first move was to find out if Remington had any knowledge of the defect prior to the accident. Our investigation included a study of all of the periodical literature on guns published since the Mohawk 600 went into production, to see if there were any published accounts of other accidents. I compiled a thick package of indexed and summarized information showing a history of problems since the 1960s.

This led to an interview with a Remington dealer in the Texas backwoods who had talked to a Remington representative about the defect years earlier. The dealer told us that Remington instructed him to simply replace any defective gun with a new one, for which Remington would reimburse him, because "we don't want to have a recall."

For business reasons, the dealer would talk only off the record, but his statement convinced me that Remington had known about the defects for years. At that point, I amended our complaint to sue several Remington officers and directors personally because of their failure to take action when they must have known there was grave danger.

Once the action was filed, the presiding judge of the court in Austin wanted to assign it to a judge who had not tried any cases with John Coates, to avoid the appearance of being partial. That was hard to do because Coates had tried cases before all of the local judges who presided at civil trials. As a solution, a criminal court judge, Thomas Blackwell, was chosen. Since he was a retired U.S. Army general, he knew something about weapons.

Remington's attorneys made a motion to force me to produce the weapon so that it could be examined by their own experts—a routine step, but one which posed a problem here. If the weapon were altered in the slightest bit, it would not perform for the jury as it had in the accident. I opposed the motion and suggested as an alternative that any examination be conducted in open court in Austin, with the judge present and a court reporter and videotape camera recording all of the proceedings. While such a procedure is common in criminal practice, for dealing with crucial physical evidence, it is not at all common in civil litigation. The defense argued that it was "unheard-of." The judge (a criminal judge, you will recall) said that, unheard-of or not, he would allow it, and the gun went into a bank vault at the plaintiff's expense until Remington could get their experts together.

On the day of the examination, the judge, reporter, camera operator, lawyers, and experts were present, and the Remington crew looked over the gun for several hours. I warned them not to remove the trigger housing or safety for any purpose, and our own expert was watching over their shoulders to be sure they made no repairs on the gun while they handled it.

At the end of the examination, the Remington experts said on camera that the gun was free of any defects. Unknown to them, my partner, Gus Kolius, had slipped a blank cartridge into the chamber after they had finished. Gus said, "Would the Remington people or the defense lawyers like to see the gun malfunction? I'd be happy to demonstrate it." He then put the rifle through its paces, and as he pushed the safety forward, the blank fired as it had with Will Coates, scattering the assembled lawyers and experts. The judge, maintaining admirable composure, asked, "Is everybody happy?"

The Remington lawyers had been offering $1 million to settle the case. After the gun had fired in the courtroom demonstration, they asked permission to visit John Coates and see his physical condition firsthand. He had been in bed, paralyzed, for nearly a year and had suffered terribly, especially from the bedsores that are the special curse of the paralysis victim. Nevertheless, being a defense lawyer, he had performed his own defense-oriented evaluation of the case and thought the million-dollar offer was appropriate.

After the defendants had taken a look at him, they raised their offer to $2.5 million but still clung to their insistence that the weapon was not defective. They reminded us of Will's anguished cry that he had shot his father, evidence, they insisted, of fault on his part. I was incensed by this and broke off the negotiations, then served subpoenas for the depositions of three Remington quality-control workers, an executive vice president, and a public relations official. Remington had ten days to get ready for these depositions (to be held in New York) and only three months before trial was scheduled to begin.

I sent Gus Kolius ahead to New York to prepare for the depositions, with instructions not to discuss a settlement. Evidently, concerned about what would develop from the depositions of the company officials, Remington decided over the course of those ten days to raise their offer to $5 million and asked Kolius to relay the figure by phone to me.

When Gus called, I told him to turn down the offer, but Gus was reluctant, and he handed the telephone over to the insurance official who was trying to negotiate the settlement. I repeated that the suit was for $7 million and that I would not settle for less. The insurance official said flatly, "I will not pay you $7 million."

I said, "Well, if you say yes before you hang up that phone, you can settle for $6.8 million and save $200,000, but if we finish without agreeing I will amend my complaint to ask for more money." After a pause of perhaps ten seconds, the insurance official, an Englishman, said, "Guv'nor, you have just settled your lawsuit!"

The $6.8 million settlement was paid at the Austin courthouse on the October 23, 1978, with reporters from newspapers and wire services in attendance. They asked me what I thought the company should do now about the Mohawk 600, and I emphasized a point that I had tried to impress on Remington during the negotiations: "If they had any decency, they would recall the damned thing."

With the money paid, the Remington attorneys asked if they could have the rifle. I said, "No, no, my friends. You purchased John Coates' cause of action, not a rifle. I have the rifle now, and you can bid on it if you want it."

The gun still belonged to Will Coates, but, of course, he never wanted to see it again. So I arranged for its repurchase at the original price of $278, plus a letter from Remington Arms to Will stating that the weapon was the entire problem and that he was in no way responsible for his father's injuries. Then, and only then, did I turn over the rifle to Remington.

John Coates recovered from his injuries sufficiently to return to his law practice on a part-time basis—in a wheelchair. Will Coates went on to play baseball and football in high school. He recovered emotionally from the wrenching experience and, if anything, the incident drew the family even closer.

The day after the settlement press conference, when I urged the company to recall the Mohawk 600, Remington gave in. They announced a nationwide recall program affecting 200,000 firearms and published notices in newspapers and magazines, similar to this one, which appeared in the January 1979 issue of *Field and Stream:*

> IMPORTANT MESSAGE TO OWNERS OF REMINGTON MODELS 600 AND 660 RIFLES, MOHAWK 600 RIFLES AND XP-100 PISTOLS—
>
> Under certain unusual circumstances, the safety selector and trigger of these firearms could be manipulated in a way that could result in accidental discharge.
>
> The installation of a new trigger assembly will remedy this situation. Remington is, therefore, recalling all Remington model 600 and 660 rifles, and all Mohawk 600 rifles—except those with a serial number starting with A.

And so on.

As for my role in the case, after I talked to the expert it was about as easy as rolling out of bed. It didn't take a lot of genius. But we did manage to litigate an unsafe rifle, a defective and dangerous product, out of circulation. The tort law process worked far more effectively to protect the public interest than did government regulations or the morals of the marketplace.

CHAPTER 6

JURIES

Years ago, I was trying a case with a good friend, Scott Baldwin, in Beaumont, which we did now and again for fun. I had made it a rule never to sit in the second chair, but with Baldwin I agreed to split it.

He was a skilled and insightful lawyer who became the president of the American Trial Lawyers Association and the International Academy of Trial Lawyers.

The jury box was to my right, the witness was on the stand, and the clock was moving toward 11:25 in the morning when I felt a tug on the back of my coat. Baldwin said, "Jamail, that juror on the end of the first row hates your guts."

I arched an eyebrow and returned my attention to the witness. "I'm not kidding," the voice behind me continued. "He's making faces at you, sticking his tongue out."

I said, "Well, what do you want me to do about it?'

Just then Judge Joe Fisher called a recess. He was a

kindly man, and we were two young lawyers he happened to like. "What's going on there?" he asked.

I said, "Lawyer Baldwin says that one of the jurors hates
me."

And the judge nodded and said, "Yeah, I noticed him
grimacing."

The jurors had filed out of the room by now, and I
shrugged. "To hell with it," I said. "Maybe he'll die." It
was just one of those things you say.

After lunch, the clerk brought the jury back in, and
there was some stirring as they took their seats. Then I
heard a thud and turned around, and the juror in question
pitched forward, thumped his head on the rail, and stayed
that way. He was dead of an apparent heart attack.

I raised my hand and started to stay something.
Baldwin locked his briefcase and took a step back: "Don't
TOUCH me," he said. "Don't even get close to me."

"Well, hell, I didn't do anything," I complained. "Why
should I feel guilty?"

The deceased juror was still bent over against the rail-
ing. No one seemed to know quite what to do. Then Judge
Fisher decided to make a speech, and he mentioned the
man's name and said—there was a little flag in his voice—
"this man has died in the service of his country." That inspired a juror to suggest that they take up a collection for
flowers. As they passed a plate, one juror put in a quarter
and took out fifteen cents in change. Judge Fisher leaned
over and whispered, "Does that tell you boys anything
about the damages in this case?"

Years later, Lee and I were riding in a car with Macey
and Harry Reasoner, a brilliant lawyer. I told the story
and Harry asked what the cause of death was.

Lee responded immediately, "Boredom, probably."
There is a possibility that he really did not like me, or he
may have been having chest pains, or he may have
thought our case stunk.

In any event, I do not pander to juries. I treat them as equals. I have seen lawyers talk to them as if they were three-year-olds, and I have reacted by telling jurors, "What you just heard is an insult to your intelligence."

Much has been said and written about my supposed rapport with juries. One of my lawyers, a twenty-year associate, David Bebout, once said, "The thing that most people don't understand about Joe Jamail is that he's weird. When I say weird, I mean like Carlos Castenada's *Teachings of Don Juan*. I am convinced that Jamail can project his will on other people. Just being near someone, he can make them feel however he wants."

I won't pretend there are not moments when spooky things go on around me, in or out of the courtroom. I also understand there is an advantage in having people think this, and say it, and for opposing attorneys to argue about it.

But there is no mystery. I don't do card tricks in front of a jury. I try to get them involved in the case, and I am not afraid to correct a mistake in front of them. I have had witnesses absolutely screw up on the stand, and I would say, "I know you're scared. Now let's go back over what you just said." I'm not really doing that for the benefit of the witness. I am doing it for the jury.

This is not engineering. The law is not an exact science. It is a living thing that changes every day, if not every hour. If something funny happens during testimony, I laugh. I don't sit there like a stone.

I was trying a case once in San Antonio, in front of Judge Murray, and the lawyer for the other side was examining a witness named Stanley Joseph Guzik, a Polish man, who claimed he was injured working on a track outside San Antonio for the Southern Pacific Railroad. He said you have to work them with your hands.

Halfway through the trial, he changed his testimony. He said there was a switch swinging back and forth, and it hit him in the testicles. I was cracking up. I said, "Mr. Guzick, the photographs show a picture of this switch. It's a manual switch, so it doesn't swing. More than that, how tall are you? Five-foot-eight? You'd have to be eleven feet tall for that switch to have hit you in the testicles." I couldn't stop laughing. The jurors were laughing. I looked up and the judge had his head buried in his robe.

When I rose for my closing argument, I said to the jury, "I know you're waiting with bated breath to hear me talk about that switch . . ."

I have this feeling when a jury comes in and looks at me. It is like a cleansing. There is a nonverbal communication: "Dammit, we didn't let them steamroller us, and now there is a bond. You did what I asked you to do on the evidence I presented to you."

So there is hope, and it springs eternal, that honesty and ability will overcome the sham and the cruelty of just denying someone their day in court. I see the torture these people go through because their whole future is at stake. Most of the clients I represent don't have any money. Not the companies, the people. They don't know how they are going to pay the rent. You take a man who has been injured and can't work anymore. He has a wife and kids. You don't just take away his job; you take away his pride. If you can't get that into a jury's heart and mind, then go be a proctologist. This is the wrong profession. A lot of people want to call that too simple a view. No, that's reality.

Their kids are worried about being able to go to the same schools, about being on welfare. It can destroy a family. If you can't share that feeling, if you can't get down to that kind of emotion, don't fake it and mess up these people's lives.

I talk to a jury on the highest plane I can because I have found that they will reach up and try to get the content of your thoughts. They know you are not a country bumpkin.

They know you went to law school. They are going to think that either you didn't learn a damned thing, or else you're trying to con them.

There are lawyers who think they have to have a different pose for everything in life. I prepare. I'm ready when I show up. I just will not have done my job if I don't. There are already too many like that: *Give me the file, I'll race over there and do my John Wayne act.* I plan all the nuances. I could do the other, and wing it, but I would probably fall on my ass.

One of the biggest mistakes some lawyers make is trying to coach the witnesses to tell something their way. The first thing I do is listen for as long as the plaintiff wants to talk. If it gets way out of hand, I'll stop it. Then I'll go through it and see what I think is important, then have a second conference with them. At that point, I'm trying in my mind to size up what kind of person they are—gregarious or shy, inward or outward, defensive, whatever. It makes a difference to me in terms of what kind of jury I want for that person. I talk to every one of the main witnesses myself.

I have a chart I use. I start doing match-ups on the defense's key witnesses and the plaintiff's key witnesses. A) Who is going to combat Big Thunder over here on the defense side? B) What are they going to say? I take their deposition. Then I make keys. I put one of the defense witnesses on and one for the plaintiff to contest what the defense witness said. I try to pair them back to back so a jury can compare and decide quickly which way they want to go, at least up to that point.

It is also helpful to me because I do not spray the jury with a shotgun, I use a rifle shot. I say, this is what they did, and I set out to prove it. I usually make a chart of twelve boxes, and in it I put the personality traits, first, over here, of the plaintiffs. And the traits of the defendant, as I see it, because I'm the one who has to go over there and do it.

Then in these twelve boxes, I will list the personality traits of a prospective juror I would like to have to assess this case. Then I have another chart of a type of personality I definitely do not want. Nothing is infallible, but at least I'm looking for certain things, the kind of personality that is going to best fit the evidence that is going to be put on by the plaintiff and the witnesses. As much as I'm looking for ones who would be favorable, I'm looking just as strongly, maybe more so, for the ones who would resent the kind of personality the defendant has, or the defendant's witnesses, or the plaintiffs.

This is how I do it, with the help of some very bright associates. I believe the jury selection, the voir dire, is the most important part of any case. I do not use jury consultants, no disrespect intended. I don't do it. I guess it works, but I can't see it. Texaco had four mock trials and the jury ruled in their favor every time. At the end, I said, "Well, who the fuck did they have playing my part?"

I'm the one looking the jurors in the eye. I know what I want. Am I going to get up there and look for something somebody else wants? I know my case better than that jury consultant. I'm not mocking them. It is just part of what I do.

I've made this point before. Courtrooms are full of lawyers who would bore people to the point that they could gag a maggot off a meat wagon. Too many times juries decide a case on the basis of which lawyer bored them the least. You can see it. Just walk over to the courthouse and look.

And you can never, ever take it for granted the jurors will like you, you sweet-talking devil. I learned this the hard way, the best way, and I never forgot it.

I had a case where a big Dallas oilman left all his money to the medical centers. His name was John Lettie Jones, and he was a devoted supporter of the Shriners

Hospital and SMU. This was so long ago, and I was so dumb, so recently out of law school, that I took the case. He left his third cousin one million dollars, and she wasn't satisfied with it and I agreed to go up there and try to break that will.

I took the case as a favor to a classmate, who had enough sense not to come to the trial, and I knew after one day that the case couldn't be won.

The judge was a Mason or a Shriner, and the jurors all had these pins in their lapels. That jury looked at me with their arms folded all through the trial. *Take that money away from those little crippled children and give it to that greedy woman?* I couldn't overcome that. They did not like me at all.

As a final gesture, the jury sent a note to the judge, asking if they could do something bad to me.

I filed that one under lessons learned. I never thought I was invincible (at least not since I was in my twenties). Still, I take seriously the fact that, for many years, I have been asked by other lawyers how to voir dire, and select a jury, and how to make closing arguments. I can tell them nothing of any value that would directly help them.

Every case is unique and every jury is unique. It all depends on the facts and the circumstances, which change from case to case: who your opponent is, the kind of case you are trying, who the judge is going to be, and factors yet unknown.

It all comes down to you, the lawyer. How do you feel about people? How deep is your understanding of them, their frailties, their strengths, their doubts, their beliefs and dreams and hopes? How do you express yourself and communicate?

In closing argument, you can't adequately express and convince a jury about pain, or any other loss, from quoting some textbook or from what some other lawyer has told you. You have to feel it, believe it, know what it does to a person in order to relate to the jury what pain or anguish has been caused to your client.

I receive hundreds of letters and phone calls asking me to take cases. They are cases of all kinds—criminal, mostly civil, pathetic, sad, foolish, impossible cases. I try to respond to each one. I accept probably one out of three hundred of these cases. Of the rest, those that have merit I try to recommend to a conscientious young lawyer.

I also get many letters and phone calls from forlorn and frustrated people who feel they have been neglected or betrayed or "sold out" by their attorneys. These are the calls that are so troublesome.

In spite of all the history we are taught, all the personal lessons we experience, we get emotional about things we cannot control. But I know we are not going to come this way again, and I am doing my best to leave a few signs along the way to help guide those who follow. I know why I took the path I took. I have been involved with the plight of my clients. I laughed with them, I cried with them, I have been happy for them, and I have been sad.

But I always tried to understand and help. I had no choice. I could never have lived with myself if it had been otherwise.

Every lawyer needs a philosophy. I am still working on mine and will keep refining it until the last breath I take.

It is particularly distressing to me when the paid hatchet men for the insurance companies, and other Chamber of Commerce types, purchase the paragons of propaganda to peddle the lie that most lawsuits are frivolous and that we need a different system than jury trials.

The message is self-explanatory. They say, "We don't trust the people to do our bidding and, after all, they are not like us. We are special. They are really peasants. The greedy, great unwashed and their lawyers have brought about a 'lawsuit explosion,' resulting in a crisis."

What they refuse to admit is that when claimants bring their grievances to court, they are saying by their actions, "We are a people who believe in law. We believe our court system has integrity and accessibility.

"When we seek help in the legislatures we are powerless, for we have no money—no political action committees. And the slumbering bureaucracies of government cannot be wakened by our pleas."

In medieval England, the then new-fangled form of alternate dispute resolution was an invention called trial by jury. It was sold as a better alternative than trial by combat, or by ordeal of fire, or by ordeal of water.

Some of our legal generation had their own alternative dispute resolution. They would meet with opposing counsel for the lunchtime conference—or cocktail conference, a legal "happy hour." After a time for tranquillity and attitude adjustment, they usually could see more merit in the opponent's case, and settlements often resulted.

To those who denigrate all lawyers, I suggest that a lawyer builds a good name, a jewel beyond price. A lawyer builds a fairer, freer, more open society. A lawyer builds truth—and justice. A lawyer named Daniel Webster told us that justice is the greatest concern of man on earth.

It is lawyers who have nurtured our constitution and kept it strong, so that when power corrupts and the crunch comes, our refuge is not mere hollow words. Many a nation without a courageous independent bar has had its strongly worded constitution emasculated by those in power. Not here, not yet, at least, for here we have the rule of law, thanks to lawyers.

We have a government of laws and not of men, thanks to lawyers.

We have a free press, thanks to lawyers.

We have police restrained by due process, thanks to lawyers.

We have judges and juries brave enough to convict an attorney general and to stare down a president until he resigned.

In spite of all the critics, I see many concerned, caring, and competent lawyers. These clamorous critics who castigate lawyers remind me of Brendan Behan's remark that a critic is like a eunuch in a harem. He has never done it himself, has never seen it done, and can't do it, but only has criticized others.

The Spanish have a proverb: It is not the same to talk about the bulls as to be in the bullring.

Today lawyers are under siege because, just as in Shakespeare's day, those who seek to sack freedom know that it is lawyers and judges who guard the bridge between freedom and tyranny.

Clarence Darrow put it straight. He said: "You can't be free if I'm not free. The place for that kind of fight—short of revolution—always has been the courtroom and the soldiers in that fight have always been trial lawyers."

(Above) What's wrong with this picture? Nothing. Behind me, first row, Denise Davidson and Elisha Kimball; second row, Janet Hansen, Donna Ramage, Jefferie Kmiec, Beth Case, Gina Adamo; third row, Melva Strahan, Jana Green, Jana Martin (hidden), Darcy McMillan, Amy Hughes, Robin Young.

(Left) Denise Davidson is my confidante and keeper of the keys. She runs the office and has for the past twenty-five years.

(Above) With Lee at my side, I've had always had a great view of the world. (Top right) With two of my favorite people, Coach Darrell Royal and Willie Nelson, after Texas defeated Alabama, in the 1973 Cotton Bowl. (Below right) With two of my friends for life, in our salad days: George Cire (middle) and Luke McConn.

(Above) With Scott Baldwin.
(Center) With Roy Cullen.
(Below) With Betty Liedtke.
(Far right) Harry Reasoner
is overcome with emotion
while presenting me with
a law school award.

George Cire wore the robe with distinction. He was my law partner, a former Marine, state district judge, appellate judge, and federal judge.

In our railroad car in Churchill, Canada, rubbing elbows with Constable Bob of the Royal Canadian Mounted Police.

We wish Jeanette McDonald and Nelson Eddy could have been there: Lee Jamail (left) and Lee Godfrey at top; Harry Reasoner, Sandy Godfrey, Joe, and Macey Reasoner, bottom row, enjoyed the Canadian sunsets.

(Above) When Willie recorded Stardust *I told him it would never sell. A million copies later, he had his platinum record framed and sent it to me with a note: "You're right, Lawyer." (Right) The Mike Campbell Golf Tournament honors the popular Texas defensive coach in the glory years of Darrell Royal (shown in the upper middle photo of this montage). Mack Brown is far left. The little man with the big chest is Rooster Andrews, the team manager who drop-kicked extra points in the Bobby Layne era.*

1999
MIKE CAMPBELL
TOURNAMENT
Sponsored By
Lee & Joe Jamail

As the sign says, I have on occasion moved my law practice to Maribell's, a favorite watering hole on Galveston Bay at Seabrook.

Elisha Kimball and Nat B. King.

HERE COME THE LONGHORNS, sprinting onto Joe Jamail Field at the Darrell K. Royal– Texas Memorial Stadium.

at sight!
_____. Thanks for
Longhorn Football.
Hook 'em Horns
Mack Brown

When asked what I thought about investment bankers, I gave the universal gesture meaning "We're number one."

BOOK TWO

THE TESTIMONY

The Match-Ups

JAMAIL: *Did Gordon Getty think you were his friend?*

TISCH: *Define* friend *for me and I'll answer the question.*

JAMAIL: *Sir, I can't define the New York friendship.*

CHAPTER 7

A MAN'S WORD

The phrase "a bet-the-company case" was the first label to stick, but there was no danger that Texaco would cease to exist, whatever the outcome. The odds were about the same as those of eradicating social diseases.

They had also referred to the looming spectacle, one not previously seen or endured in big business or big oil or even big snake oil, as "the most important business case ever brought in the history of America."

Do you know who *they* were? Me. I said it, and during the trial, I believed it.

What was a man's honor worth, or a promise, or a handshake? Either the law did not sanction stealing and old values mattered, or dealmaking would revert to the rule of the Old West, where the one with the fastest horse or the fastest draw won.

True, I was prejudiced. I believed in my client and his claim. Lawyers are not paid to be neutral.

Pennzoil sued Texaco for fraudulently inducing Getty Oil to break a contract that would have given Pennzoil a billion barrels of choice oil reserves. The trial would last five and a half months, result in 25,000 pages of transcript, and conclude with a verdict ninety times larger than the greatest judgment ever to survive an appeal.

I knew we would win the case. I just didn't know exactly how. I had been involved in cases of corporate fraud, but not a big money merger, or a takeover, hostile or friendly. So those were some of my advantages.

But the story needs to start at the beginning, which means in my version it needs to start with J. Hugh Liedtke, born in Tulsa in 1922, a law graduate of the University of Texas, a man who founded Zapata Oil with an aspiring politician named George Herbert Walker Bush. Liedtke later founded Pennzoil and dedicated himself to turning it into one of the majors, able to compete with Exxon and Mobil and, yes, Texaco.

Liedtke and I lived close by each other in Houston and had traveled the world together with our wives, his Betty and my Lee. On New Year's Eve of 1984, Hugh had dinner at our home and asked me to wish him luck. He was leaving for New York in the morning to close, he said, "the biggest deal of his lifetime," and maybe anyone's lifetime in the oil patch, and that was all he could say about it. Betty was in Hawaii with their daughters.

I said, "That's all I want to know about it."

A few days later, I heard on the news that Pennzoil had made a deal to acquire three-sevenths of Getty Oil. I was happy for Liedtke. The next thing I knew, he called from his room at the Waldorf Astoria and shouted into the phone, "I have just been cheated out of Getty Oil by Texaco. They have stolen a billion barrels of our oil!"

I stopped him right there, told him not to say another word, to pack his bags and come home. I felt flattered that he had called me in his moment of distress. But I knew he had several law firms representing him, including Baker Botts, of Houston, and Paul Weiss, of New York.

When Hugh had returned to Houston, Gus Kolius and I went to his office. Gus was a helluva lawyer. I have never known a better one. He was valuable to me in every way, including curbing my temper or my impulsiveness when I needed curbing.

He is more than a good influence, of course. He is the complete lawyer. He knows more about the subject he is addressing than the expert he is examining. He is the best lawyer I have ever tried a case against, and we tried three. He won the first, I won the second, and the third was settled. He was and is my friend.

Liedtke and Baine Kerr, who was the president of Pennzoil and a lawyer, laid out what they saw as their grounds for an action against Texaco. I offered my first reaction. I said, "Hugh, I think you ought to forget it. If you do this, it is going to be costly and drawn out and it's going to come down to your word against theirs."

He said, "I'm not going to forget it, and I want you to take this case for me."

Later, Gus and I were walking back to our office and he said, dead serious, "Joe, don't do it. This case can't be won, and it's the quickest way I know to lose a friend."

I said, "Gus, I've told him. I've warned him. But if he asks me again I'm going to do it. He has a case. It's not frivolous. It's just damned difficult."

The next week, Lee and I joined the Liedtkes at their ranch in Arkansas. I had waited to see if he would cool off, and he hadn't. I needed to see and measure his resolve. If I was going to stick my tail in the arena, I needed a player I knew would go the distance.

We were riding around in his Land Rover, and Betty said, "Joe, he really wants you to do this."

I said, "Betty, this is a case that might never get settled. Either way, it's going to be a bloodbath."

She said, "So be it. You know he will do his share of the bleeding."

I said, "Okay, let's do it."

On Monday I was huddled with John Jeffers, a brainy forty-one-year-old Yale and University of Texas law school graduate, a partner at Baker Botts, who was working on the closing documents for Pennzoil when Texaco swept in and made its midnight raid.

I told John I was getting in the case and I hoped he had no objection. He laughed and said how proud he would be to work with me. He also said that Hugh Liedtke had called and told them that he wanted me to be the lead counsel for Pennzoil and that was just fine with him and Baker Botts.

The suit already had been filed in Delaware, and I knew, by God, we needed to dismiss that. As I have often said, I could not have done this without the great effort and legal help provided by the Baker Botts firm. There was John Jeffers, Irv Terrell, who was like a bulldog, Randy Hopkins, and Susan Roehm. Jim Kronzer, known as "the Fat Man," a nickname I gave him with affection, was recognized as the best appellate lawyer in the state.

Texaco had made the first major mistake by not filing a reply, which allowed us to dismiss the case and file it in Houston. I could have tried the case in Switzerland, but I was not going to Delaware to try it in front of some jaded corporate judge. Texaco was a Delaware company. Pennzoil was a Delaware company. So we were free to bring the suit in state court because there was no federal jurisdiction.

And for all the howling that was going to take place about home cooking, Texas juries, and Texas judges, Texaco had four times as many employees in this state as Pennzoil had.

The case was going to get ugly and nasty, and you could hardly ask for anything more. The first volley from

Dick Miller, who had been a partner at Baker Botts before starting his own small firm, was to accuse me of trying to influence the judge, Anthony P. Farris, with a campaign contribution for $10,000. I had made a pledge in October at the request of Joe Reynolds, another old friend and former Marine, who wouldn't take a fee for his work on one of my cases and asked me instead to help his friend. I wrote the check before Judge Farris had been assigned to the case.

There was a full-fledged hearing, and a visiting judge threw out the accusation. I thought the whole episode was nonsense. You don't bribe a judge by writing him a check. You give him cash, in an envelope, on the golf course. At least, that was what Federal Judge Charles Brieant, of New York, said when Texaco brought it up at a bond hearing.

Besides, one of Texaco's lawyers was a member of Judge Farris' reelection finance committee, which solicited the money they got from me. But that set the tone for much of the fencing and the courtroom dramatics, as well.

For weeks, an hour at a time, or half an hour, or ten minutes, I walked around my desk and fantasized about the case. I looked at the chart I always prepared to pick the twelve jurors. I asked myself who would be the key witnesses. Obviously, Hugh Liedtke would play a prominent role, and Baine Kerr and our expert, Dr. Thomas Barrow, who had been the chairman of Sohio, a University of Texas grad with a doctorate from Stanford, a man with terrific credentials. He had also been an executive vice president of Exxon.

Then it hit me. Our key people were not going to be from Pennzoil. The Texaco witnesses were the ones who would win the case for us. I had gone over and over the facts of how the story had unfolded, and I was dry washing my hands at the prospect of questioning all of the lawyers and bankers who had thrown the first grenades.

There was the Texaco chairman, John K. McKinley, Gordon Getty, Marty Siegel, a New York investment banker, Marty Lipton, the lawyer for the Getty Museum, and Laurence Tisch, a Getty director.

The two key players in this morality play, as I saw it, were Lipton, who was a savvy takeover lawyer, and McKinley. I knew I had to peel the skin off Lipton. To create the effect I wanted, I needed to find the jurors with the right personality traits, who would most resent the conduct of Texaco and its power brokers and were more likely to relate to Liedtke and Kerr and their supporters.

The biggest hurdle we had to overcome was the fact that the final papers had not been signed. But the chronology was not open to dispute. Our position was:

On January 3, 1985, the Getty Oil board of directors, by a 15-to-1 vote, agreed to a merger with Pennzoil.

The next day, Getty's investment banking firm presented its bill for the deal it had negotiated with Pennzoil.

On January 5, Gordon Getty's attorney told a California judge that there was a "transaction presently agreed upon" between Getty Oil and Pennzoil. Getty's investment banker filed a court affidavit to the same effect.

On the evening of the fifth, while lawyers for Pennzoil and Getty worked out the details of the formal merger agreement, Texaco's chairman of the board secretly met with Gordon Getty and offered to purchase the stock for a higher price ($125 a share, later raised to $128) than Pennzoil had offered.

As part of its agreement to purchase Getty, Texaco promised to indemnify all involved with Getty Oil against any lawsuit Pennzoil might bring for breach of contract.

I had already decided that I would try this case not as a matter of securities law, or fiduciary duty, or any other issue of the takeover game, but as a matter of honor. I would ask the jury to send a message that the public demanded a higher standard of behavior from Wall Street and its giant corporations.

This was not the way most corporate lawyers would want to try such a case. It was surely not the way Texaco wanted to try it—dancing a minuet. I planned to hammer the point that Texaco stole this oil from Pennzoil and that made the company no better than a thief. When you take something that belongs to someone else, it's theft.

On the makeup of the jury, I would change my thinking from time to time, day to day. Did I want someone aggressive or passive? There was little science to it. I called on all my experience from childhood on, things I learned from my mother, everything good and bad that ever happened to me.

I had to make this a confrontation between people if I was going to convey any emotion to a jury that would pique their interest. Contract law is not exciting to me or anybody else except some crazed human being who looks at that crud all the time.

I knew in my mind that Texaco would never settle. They had a very savvy, seasoned, starchy trial lawyer, Dick Miller, who was not the settling kind. Both sides agreed on a fast track. We went to trial in sixteen months from the day it was filed, and in a case of this kind that is fast.

We had a two-week delay when Judge Farris became ill and could not continue. He was replaced by a visiting judge, Solomon Casseb. That had no bearing on anything. My concern was that the jury not lose the rhythm of the case.

Hell, I had known Dick Miller for forty years. He was another ex-Marine, one tough act. We got extremely hostile with each other because every day was going to be a war. He had been a trial lawyer at Baker Botts and I knew his techniques. Dick was abrasive almost to the point of being abusive. He gave no quarter and tried to run roughshod over anyone he could. But I knew something else.

Dick had once represented me in a libel suit. One of the people involved was a state legislator, Jack Ogg. My insurance company called, and I said I wanted Miller to handle it.

Anyone who thinks Dick Miller is not an excellent trial lawyer has never had to try a case against him. Dick did one of the cleverest things I had seen. Ogg had claimed I damaged his reputation, and when Miller took his deposition he handed him a yellow pad and a pencil. He asked him to write down the name of every person who thought less of him now than they did before, and he gave him fifteen minutes. This was being videotaped. When we came back, the legal pad was blank. Dick said, "Hmmm, this must have been written in lemon juice."

So Miller was no stranger to me. I knew that if I could force him to play catch-up, our chances of winning would be improved. That was the advantage I had starting the voir dire, because Texaco must have made fifteen motions for mistrial before we finished. That was his style. He had a military bearing, rigid, clothes cut tight, standing erect. I'm instinctive, loose, relaxed. I will sometimes laugh out loud in the courtroom, causing people to stare at me, because laughter there is rare. But it isn't a morgue. Anyway, we offered a stark contrast.

CHAPTER 8

MAKING THE CASE

Once Hugh Liedtke had made his intentions known, by announcing in New York that he would be suing "everyone involved," he was a man relatively calm and at peace with himself.

In the end, we were suing only one defendant, Texaco, and in this case one was enough. We were taking dead aim at the company that had service stations in all fifty states; the company that sponsored Bob Hope and Milton Berle, and whose motto had been, "You can trust your car to the man with the star."

I grew more eager and more confident by the day. I looked ahead to seating the jury as though it was going to be a national holiday.

And Hugh Liedtke, this robust, barrel-chested former Navy officer, sometime lawyer, hard-nosed oilman, and fierce competitor, had no clue as to what my strategy would be. John Jeffers and Irv Terrell, my co-counsel from Baker

145

Botts, would often look at me and ask, "When are we going to settle on our approach?" Of course, it kept shifting. I would say to Hugh over a drink, "I think I will do such-and-such," and he would just shrug.

While I was in Galveston, thinking about this case, a strategy was beginning to take shape in my mind.

At first, it was elusive and shadowy. A few days later, I began thinking about the instructions the judge would be giving the jury at the start of the case and again at the end. This was strange ground for me, because I had tried so many cases this was an automatic reflex, done subconsciously in my preparations.

One of the instructions to be given seemed to return repeatedly: "You are the judges of the credibility of the witnesses ... keep an open mind until all the evidence is in."

I knew this was going to be a long trial. It would take months. How was I going to keep the jury focused on the matters I knew to be important? I had to put the Pennzoil case on first; the defendant, Texaco, would follow. Wouldn't the jury forget what Pennzoil witnesses said? Wouldn't the Texaco witnesses cause doubt and confusion? This was troublesome. It was then that the elusive, shadowy images that had been bothering me became clear.

I would cast the case in a way that the jury would decide the credibility of the witnesses on the spot.

I decided then that I had to revise our order of proof and put on the Texaco person regarding the issue that person was going to be testifying about, then immediately follow him or her with a Pennzoil witness who would testify about the same issue. In that way, the jurors would make up their minds about that issue then, at that time, not later.

I was confident that I could put the Texaco witnesses on adversely and make the jury see those witnesses through my questions instead of favorable, friendly questions Texaco's lawyers would ask them. I also knew that I would have thoroughly prepared Pennzoil's witnesses so that the match-up, back to back, would turn out well for Pennzoil.

I was right. So in my mind, that strategy became "The Match-up": Marty Lipton against Arthur Liman, Blaine Kerr against James Kinnear, Hugh Liedtke against John McKinley.

The case was shaping up as more fun than I had thought. I had flown to New York to depose McKinley and turned around and went home the next day, totally satisfied. He was surrounded by his executives and lawyers, who seemed openly frightened by what I might do to him. Here was a man who was the chief executive officer of one of the largest corporations in the world, and he could barely look me in the eye.

I noticed that when he was about to say something transparently untruthful, he had a habit of turning his head. This was why I preferred to do my own depositions of key witnesses. How else would I learn what signals they were giving away?

We were only minutes into his deposition when McKinley, a pinched, austere-looking man, was almost tongue-tied. I had asked him if his responsibilities as chairman of Texaco included the power to "bind" his company to a contract. Richard Keeton, one of Miller's partners, advised him not to answer.

I asked McKinley if he understood the question. Again, Keeton instructed him not to answer. I tugged at my sleeve and said, "I think I will look at this watch."

"You are browbeating the witness," wailed Miller.

"Sit down," I said. "I have not started the browbeating."

"Cut the crap and get on with it," said Miller.

I asked McKinley if he thought an agreement meant a meeting of minds. And he was told not answer.

"I am asking his opinion as an expert," I said.

"He is not an expert," Miller retorted.

I was frankly amazed. I turned to McKinley and said, "Your counsel is claiming that you don't know how to do your job."

"You are so unfair," Miller chimed in, disgust in his voice.

I again addressed McKinley: "Are you going to take the Fifth Amendment on that?"

Miller was chagrined. "That is such a chickenshit remark."

"I do not care what you think," I snorted.

At that point, Irv Terrell, of Baker Botts, who had been groomed as a young attorney by Miller, broke in: "You have a short fuse, Dick."

"Shut your mouth," Miller said. "You better be careful."

"You better make me," said Terrell. "You have a hell of a short fuse."

This was like the orchestra warming up before the concert. All the way back to Houston I felt a rising sense of excitement. I was certain the Texaco lawyers would not risk putting McKinley on the stand, but I felt there was serious mileage to be gained from his deposition.

I spent the two weeks before the trial at our beach house in Galveston, Texas. I was alone. The house has a wide, magnificent view of the beach and the Gulf of Mexico. I did this to be able to totally concentrate, without distraction. It was here that I made the final decision on the order of witnesses and the style and procedure that we would use to present the case. I also focused completely on each of the main witnesses, one at a time, and then how to make each witness fold into every other witness in that area.

I spent three of those days concentrating on what type of jurors we wanted and how I would handle the language, the questions I would ask and the ones I anticipated the jurors asking—all of the nuances that go into voir dire and jury selection.

Jury selection is a difficult task. The case had been given wide publicity nationally. Feelings were running so high on both sides that it was going to be difficult to seat jurors who had not formed an opinion about the case. My belief about jurors is what it is about people generally. I believe no one is wholly good or wholly bad. We all have our weaknesses and strengths. My duty as a trial lawyer is to try to discover those traits and address them so that I can best represent my client.

Texaco's entire top brass showed up in court for what everyone expected to be the first day of jury selection. But the length of the disagreements over protocol forced the judge to send the jury pool home until the next day. As I looked around the courtroom, I could not believe my eyes. There in a front-row seat was John McKinley. His lawyers did not plan to put him on the stand, and we could not compel his appearance because the subpoena power of state courts in Texas ranged for only one hundred miles.

But they had felt safe in having him attend so that the jurors could see him sort of waving the flag. Now here he was right in our laps.

The honor of serving him went to Susan Roehm, a perky young associate from Baker Botts. "Hi, Mr. McKinley," she said brightly. "I haven't seen you since the depositions in New York." As he returned her smile, she slapped a subpoena into his outstretched hand, making him a witness, after all—for Pennzoil.

When we received the jury list, I found myself listening to everybody. Lawyers are funny. Once you have taken the lead, you cannot allow yourself to be drawn into a debating society. If you have done your homework, the Holy Spirit isn't going to fall on you.

When I was cutting the jury, I had Irv Terrell, John

Jeffers, Jim Kronzer, Liedtke, and Kerr all giving me suggestions. Finally I said, "Bullshit. Thank you for your advice," and I picked up the list and went to the toilet, where I go in every moment of crisis. I locked myself in one of the stalls and just stood there and struck it by myself.

There were two characteristics I was looking for, loyalty and honesty. Why? When you give your word, that brings in your loyalty. I could prove that the Getty board was disloyal to J. Paul Getty, who had founded the company. I wanted jurors who had longevity in marriage, longevity in job, longevity in church.

I came as close to hitting my charts and diagrams as one could possibly hope. We had one author; one lady who owned her own insurance company, who had been married for forty-seven years; a black postal worker married to the same woman for thirty-six years; six with college degrees; a foreman with a college degree; and the manager of a company that did business with Texaco and Pennzoil.

When I began the process I told them, "This is a case of promises, and what those promises meant to Pennzoil, and what they ultimately meant to Texaco. The question that you are going to have to decide is what a promise is worth, what your word is worth, what a handshake is worth, what a contract is worth. Because that's what a contract is: a promise."

I told them that Hugh Liedtke had gone from triumph to betrayal "because of a conspiracy between New York lawyers and New York investment bankers. You are going to see them eye to eye. You size them up."

After picking the jury, I stopped by the Liedtkes' house on my way home. Betty Liedtke, whom I loved dearly (and miss sorely) asked me what I thought about the jury. I said I liked them. She made a funny face and said sarcastically, "I'm glad you do."

Once we started calling witnesses, I had an adrenaline

rush. But there was still one huge test to be met. It always has been my policy to be balls-out when it came to introducing our figure for damages. No mincing, no ducking, no bobbing and weaving.

To make a jury understand not only the loss of income, but the pain and psychological damage to a person paralyzed or disfigured was one thing. To put a price on the loss of Hugh Liedtke's once-in-a-lifetime deal was clearly another. But in some ways I thought the task would be simpler. You could lay it out for the jury in black and white, which is exactly what we did.

We brought out an exhibit five feet tall and emblazoned with bold black lettering. Two Pennzoil executives took turns explaining the numbers from the witness stand.

This was the formula:

It would have cost Pennzoil $3.4 billion for those billion barrels, including the share of Getty Oil's debt that Pennzoil would have assumed. One billion barrels was a nice round number for the jury to ponder; it made the arithmetic simple. It worked out that Pennzoil would have gotten the those barrels for $3.40 each.

With the deal destroyed, Liedtke could replace those barrels in only one way: by going out and drilling from scratch. Even if he succeeded in locating that much oil—a doubtful prospect in the picked-over fields of America—it would cost, on the average, $10.87 for every barrel found, based on Pennzoil's experience of the previous five years.

The $10.87 figure for each replacement barrel, minus the $3.40 for each of the Getty Oil barrels, equaled $7.47 in lost opportunity.

Multiply $7.47 a barrel by one billion, 1.008 billion barrels to be exact, and we had our damages, seven billion, five hundred and thirty million dollars. We asked for the identical amount in punitive damages.

We had a bit of bad luck before we could put the figure before the jury. Our first expert witness died. But then we were fortunate to enlist Tom Barrow, with his impeccable credentials, including his membership in the Woods Hole Oceanographic Institution, part of the team that found the *Titanic*. Best of all, he was an unpaid witness.

When he was asked what arrangement for compensation he had made with Pernnzoil for his testimony he answered, "None." I saw some of the jurors straighten up in their seats.

"And why was that?"

"First of all," he replied, "I was not interested in being a professional expert witness. Second, I felt that the issue of contract law was a matter of principle as far as I was concerned, and therefore I was willing to do it on that basis." A larger-than-life oilman with no connection to the case was doing it out of principle. He was a trial lawyer's dream.

The Texaco legal team then made a judgment call that would still be debated years later. With three experts of their own standing by, they elected to call none of them and not to answer Pennzoil's claim for damages. We had fully documented our figure. Texaco offered no evidence in rebuttal. Miller said he did not want to dignify our claim by refuting it. But as one juror said when the trial had ended, "It isn't our place to fabricate a case for Texaco."

We continued to have a field day with their witnesses. Eagerly, I approached Marty Lipton, the lawyer for the Getty Museum and takeover artist.

Q. Mr. Lipton, you seem to be a man who uses his words precisely—do you?

A. I try to.

Q. Did I understand you earlier to testify that not one of your clients ever intended to be bound prior to signing a definitive merger agreement? And you meant it when you said it?

A. Yes.

Q. (I pick up a three-page document.) Were you involved in the acquisition by Esmark of Norton Simon? Although there was not a definitive merger agreement, it went through.

A. Yes, sir.

Q. Sir?

A. Yes, sir.

Q. All right, sir. Now let's talk for a minute about Mr. Siegel. Would you say Mr. Siegel is a man who uses words precisely, correctly?

A. Yes.

Q. And Mr. Siegel is a knowledgeable man in the mergers and acquisitions trade?

A. Yes.

Q. And a man who would not use words foolishly—if under oath, especially?

A. That's correct.

Q. (I hand him a copy of Plaintiff's Exhibit 19—the California court affidavit that Siegel filed after the Getty Oil board had voted on the Pennzoil deal.) Would you read it aloud, please?

(The jury hears once again how Getty's board had approved the Pennzoil deal, only this time from the mouth of Marty Lipton.) Mr. Lipton, he used the words "transaction now agreed upon," didn't he?

A. Yes, he did.

Q. Well, do you believe that he knew what he was saying?

A. No.

Q. You just disagree, is that it?

A. I disagree.

Q. You've never been shown this, have you?

A. I have not.

Q. (From behind me, I could hear Dick Miller snap at Richard Keeton, "Tell Lipton to get rid of that fucking pocket handkerchief.") You're paid large amounts of money to go and advise these people?

A. That's correct.

Q. To make sure they don't succumb to pressure?

A. That's correct.

Q. You felt terribly pressured?

A. Yes, I did.

Q. *You* didn't crater, did you?

A. I hope not.

Q. Are you telling this jury that you, who pride yourself as being the leading takeover lawyer in the country, could not prevent that board from just *cratering* because of this "assault" by Pennzoil? Are you telling us that these sixteen board members with their lawyers, their advisors—all sophisticated men, educated people who have pressures every day—succumbed to Pennzoil's pressure and voted fifteen to one on the counterproposal that they themselves made?

A. No, I don't think the pressure by Pennzoil motivated them. I think what—

Q. That answered the question.

Any trial lawyer worth his fee is willing to abandon even the most carefully planned line of questioning to seize a small piece of testimony and enlarge it into something the jury will not forget. Just such an opportunity arose when Lipton testified that in his opinion Gordon Getty could never have completed the Pennzoil deal without hiring lawyers who specialized in complex oil and gas transactions.

Q. Are you saying that two people cannot agree unless they hire a bunch of lawyers to *tell* them they've agreed?

A. I'm not saying that at all, Mr. Jamail. I'm saying that two people who are contemplating an agreement with respect to a ten-billion-dollar transaction would be awfully foolish to do it on the basis of an outline and the absence of an expert's advice . . .

Q. Mr. Lipton, are you saying that you have some distinctions between just us ordinary people making contracts with each other, and whether or not it's a ten-billion-dollar deal? Is there a different standard in your mind?

A. Yes, indeed.

I waited a full five seconds to let that response sink in. I glanced at the jury box and saw eyes get big and a jaw or two drop.

Q. Oh, I see. So, if it wasn't a bunch of money involved in this Getty–Pennzoil thing, it could be an agreement?

A. Well, if there was five or ten dollars involved, I guess you might say that.

As far as the jury was concerned, Marty Lipton had just made honor in business contingent on the number of dollars involved.

He is a smart lawyer, but I will remember that cross-examination like a bullfight. Even while I was doing it, I felt that way, nicking him, nailing him. *I've got you bleeding now, Marty, and I can kill you any time I want.* It was fun.

But, respectfully, I must say that Marty Lipton in my opinion is the best acquisition lawyer in America.

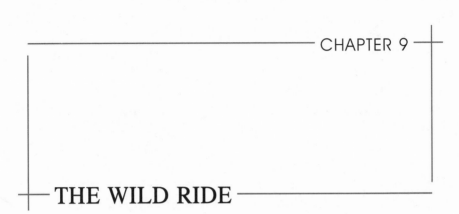

CHAPTER 9

THE WILD RIDE

I believe in matchups—as strongly as any basketball or football coach or any *yenta,* I believe in them.

That was why I put Arthur Liman, Pennzoil's New York attorney, a smooth and unassuming fellow, on the stand before Marty Lipton. And it was definitely why I wanted Hugh Liedtke back to back with John McKinley.

Liedtke charmed the jurors with his tales of drilling 127 wells back in Midland without ever encountering a dry hole, and during much of that time his partner was George Bush, whose present job was vice president of the United States. Hugh scored more points when he mentioned the appearance of J. Paul Getty at a party in Tulsa to celebrate Liedtke's engagement to Betty, countering Texaco's claim that he was an "interloper."

The illness of Judge Farris, and his replacement by Judge Casseb, caused a ten-day interruption of my questioning of Marty Lipton. The days passed quickly, since I was not yet finished with him.

Before the break, I had asked him about a memorandum of agreement that had been signed by his client, Harold Williams, the president of the Getty Museum. Williams had also offered a motion to accept the Pennzoil proposal, as David Copley, the secretary of the board meeting, reported in his notes.

I asked him about a young woman I referred to as his partner in the purchase of the museum shares. Lipton corrected me. "You said Ms. Vlahakis was my partner. She's my *associate*."

You could tell that he saw my eyes light up. He had committed a serious blunder. Lipton not only had slighted someone he worked with, a young woman, but she was pregnant at that.

One of the more active jurors, Jim Shannon, who would write a book about the case, recalled later: "When I heard that, I realized that Marty Lipton had just reinstated the caste system."

I moved on to Harold Williams' motion to accept the proposal. Lipton said, "I told them I wanted it clearly understood that the museum would be a signatory to such a plan only for the purpose of having it approved—I mean, I'm sorry, I said approved. Only for the purpose of having it considered. This whole plan was not something the museum wanted at all."

I found that statement incredible, the suggestion that his client would move to adopt a plan he did not support. "Did somebody force him to make the motion?"

"No, what Mr. Williams did was move to approve going forward with negotiations and discussions with Pennzoil."

I glanced again at my copy of Dave Copley's notes. "Was Mr. Copley sober when he was taking these notes?"

"I don't know, sir. I don't know."

Another juror, the foreman, Rick Lawler, said he thought Lipton had come across as a brilliant lawyer who fell apart when forced to deal with the real world—"a genius who can't tie his shoes."

After the ten-day delay to allow for the switching of the judges, Richard Keeton warned Lipton, "The jury thinks you're fencing. Just answer the questions yes or no."

He was dead white meat by then, and the fight had gone out of him. The indemnity clause in the Texaco contract referred to the Pennzoil agreement. I said, "You are a precise man. You could have had that language stricken, couldn't you?"

"Yes," he replied, and with that he had, in a sense, conceded that Pennzoil had a deal, after all.

Having bled Lipton, I decided to be gentle with Laurence Tisch, one of the Getty directors, who was now engaged in a takeover of CBS.

I asked him about the champagne toast he had joined in when Gordon and Ann Getty were celebrating with Hugh Liedtke the closing of the deal. He argued that they were merely toasting the acceptance of a price that could lead to an agreement later.

"You're not friends with Gordon Getty?" I pressed him.

"No, sir."

"Did Gordon Getty think you were his friend?"

"Define *friend* for me and I'll answer the question."

That was too big an opening to resist. "Sir," I replied, "I can't define the New York friendship."

Very early in the trial, we had introduced an exhibit. It was a bill from Getty's investment bankers. Instinct made me keep a copy in my secret trial notebook. I believed it would become important. It did.

I proved that Mr. Tisch was quite knowledgeable about when investment bankers submit a bill to their client. He was nasty to me and volunteered that they work on a percentage of the total amount of the deal, but not nearly as big a percentage as "your charge, Mr. Jamail." I let it slide. I dragged out the questions.

"When do they send the bill?" I asked.

He said, "After the deal is done."

I said, "Well, sometimes, they send it before an agreement is reached."

He said, "Are you deliberately not understanding, or is it just too much for you?" He went on: "They wouldn't know what to charge if the deal had not been done."

I asked, "Are you sure?"

He looked at me as though he believed me to be demented.

"Is that your sworn testimony?"

"Yes."

Then I handed him the exhibit. It was the bill to Getty from its investment bankers. "What is that, Mr. Tisch?"

He said, "It is a bill from the Getty investment bankers."

I said, "Read it aloud, Mr. Tisch."

He said in a low voice, "January fourth . . ."

I said, "Louder, Mr. Tisch." He read it again.

I said, "That looks like what you described as a done deal."

A total hush fell over the courtroom. He had earlier sworn that as a present member of the Getty board of directors, he and the others had not voted to accept the Pennzoil deal. He had been sandbagged into the truth.

Now it was time to move on to John McKinley. I would keep him squirming on the stand for a week, but all I really wanted to do was establish that Texaco had actual knowledge of the Pennzoil deal, a requirement in proving malice. I had put him on the stand as a hostile witness.

We quickly established that McKinley had a duty as

chief executive officer to make sure that Texaco's lawyers and investment bankers abided by the company's policies.

"Is it Texaco's policy, sir, to interfere with other people's contracts?"

"No," he replied.

"All right, sir, we'll come back to that."

I reminded the jurors that Liedtke had testified that a company's top management, not its lawyers, negotiated contracts. And it was McKinley himself who had made the offer to Gordon Getty in his suite at the Hotel Pierre, where two days earlier the Gettys had shared a toast about the deal.

"The lawyers don't make the definitive agreement, do they?" I prodded. "It's the top executives, such as yourself, that bind the company. Isn't that correct?"

He hesitated, looking for a trap door, but finally said, "Yes."

I put the questions to him in a way that gave him little or no leeway in his answers. "You knew that Gordon Getty and the museum had signed a memorandum of agreement?" Yes. "You could have stopped your deal when you found out?" Yes.

"You didn't do that, did you?"

"I didn't halt anything."

"And that was intentional? You did it and you knew what you were doing?"

He hemmed and hawed but finally answered, "Yes."

"Texaco's success, very simply, defeated this arrangement that Pennzoil had with Getty," I said. It was a statement, not a question, and although the answer was obvious it was not one that McKinley was anxious to give. "Is your answer 'Yes, it did'?" I finally demanded.

"Well, you just keep using the word 'defeat.' We weren't out to defeat Pennzoil and we were out—"

At this point, Judge Casseb jumped in: "Answer the question yes or no and then explain."

"The answer to your question was, I suppose, yes."

McKinley kept trying to avoid incriminating himself by tailgating his answers and slipping in the idea that everyone he talked to at Getty Oil assured him they were free to deal.

Also, McKinley had sudden short-term memory losses. Every day fifty copies of the *Wall Street Journal* were delivered to the Texaco offices, but he could not remember reading the story that on January 5, 1985, said that Pennzoil had reached an agreement to buy Getty Oil. Somehow, no one at Texaco's corporate headquarters read the *Wall Street Journal* that day.

I finally asked him if he remembered anyone at Getty referring to the situation as a "bird in the hand."

No, he didn't. I asked him if he knew what that might have meant. No, he didn't. I asked if he knew what the phrase "a bird in the hand" meant. No, he didn't know.

That was when I saw everyone in the jury box physically, bodily, turn away from him. I went on to make him admit everything—that what Texaco did was willful, intentional, knowing. I felt better after that.

On September 18, 1985, nine weeks after the jurors had first assembled, I turned to Judge Casseb and declared, "Your Honor, at this time I rest Pennzoil's case."

Now it was Texaco's turn, but I knew Dick Miller and the rest of his team would be punting from their own end zone. We had proved that hands had been shaken, that a host of documents had been signed, if not a final one, that the board of Getty Oil had approved an agreement by a vote of fifteen to one, and that Gordon and the museum had asked for indemnities against a lawsuit by Pennzoil.

I had made whatever reputation I had by convincing juries to send messages to corporate America—to build safer cars, safer guns, more reliable medicines, better drilling rigs. I always told the jury that the way to send a message was to render the kind of punishment that companies easily understand—big money judgments, because in their greed the only thing that mattered to them was the money.

The Baker Botts lawyers and the Pennzoil executives were confident, but I knew none of them believed the case was in the bag. Already, an in-house Pennzoil lawyer was drawing up dual press releases announcing a loss as well as a victory.

The outcome seemed sufficiently up in the air that just before I rose to give my closing argument, Jim Kronzer slipped me a note that contained just one word: "Cool." At first, I wondered what was cool. I grinned quizzically at Jim across the table, and I realized he was gently reminded me to contain myself. "I don't want to put any heat on you," he said softly, "but this thing is up for grabs."

Still, I knew there was only one way to bring in the gusher that Texaco feared—to arouse the jury's passion against Texaco and embolden it to award billions of dollars, a thunderbolt of a judgment.

For only the second time in my career, Lee was sitting in the courtroom.

This is the *Reader's Digest* condensed version of my closing argument. Like the sinner who gave his confession to a priest, knowing time was short, I will only hit the highlights:

"There were so many misstatements in what Mr. Miller told you that I'm not going to try to answer all of them. He starts out by giving you four hours of excuses for Texaco's conduct and he ends it by saying to you, 'Don't take away our company, because if something went wrong, it was Getty that did it.

"They bought and paid for this lawsuit when they gave the indemnities!

"Judge Casseb is one of the most honored and brilliant

judges in America. If he had wanted to say to you, 'contract,' he would have said it. I have no quarrel with [the absence] of 'contract,' but it's his charge, not Mr. Miller's.

"Some of Pennzoil's witnesses may not have told the same pat story. *He* didn't have that trouble [a nod toward Miller]. Every witness they brought reminds me of one of those squeeze dolls. You squeeze it, it says, 'Free to deal, free to deal, free to deal . . .

"They spent a lot of time by their own admission with these witnesses. They had no choice but to come in and give you some suggestive after-the-fact opinion. That's what they did. I suppose we have to start with Mr. Bart Winokur and Mr. Geoff Boisi back in Houston. You remember Back Door Bart? Snuck in the back door when they got Gordon Getty out of the room? Kicked him off, or tried to instigate a lawsuit to kick him off the board of his own family trust.

"Then there was Marty Lipton. To him, money is the object. That's what it is. That's what he said. He says people can agree without lawyers, but in his mind the amount of money makes the difference. And that's that specialized group calling themselves mergers and acquisition lawyers, carving up corporate America to their liking. They get together. They're all within a couple of miles of each other. One wins one day and another wins another day—and the investment bankers win *all* the days and *they win with these indemnities.*"

I had notes but never referred to them, except to quote a passage from the testimony. If my closing argument at times seemed to ramble or break off in fragments, there is no point in trying to pretty it up here, to connect or rearrange the thoughts. It came from places inside me and, frankly, the words appeared to work.

"Again," I continued, "if Judge Casseb wanted to say 'written contract,' he knows how to do that. He didn't. The law requires no such burden of us.

"Stop the train! They didn't stop it. They derailed it, blew it up. I thought you were going to throw up listening to all the depositions you had to hear . . .

"There has been no dispute about damages in this case. None. Texaco, through its lawyers, does not think you will assess those kinds of damages. They think you are not big enough to do that. I think you are."

One by one, I looked the jurors in the eyes. I thought to myself, "They are throwing away all the bullshit after four and a half months."

"Hugh Liedtke is my friend. Baine Kerr is my friend. And I can't divorce myself from that. But I can't divorce myself from these facts, either. They honestly endeavored to build their company.

"Hugh Liedtke, who got started with the help of J. Paul Getty . . . you heard the testimony. The man who came to his wedding party! Liedtke, a stranger, an interloper, going to rape that company? He got his start from that family! Believed he could work with them—and he could have, if it had not been sabotaged.

"You people here, you the jury, are the conscience, not only of this community now in this hour, but of this country. What you decide is going to set the standard of morality in business in America for years to come . . .

"There is no half justice without half injustice. Don't compromise your morals or your verdict. They think you are not big enough to send this message. I'm not. The court is not. You are. Only you. You can turn a cold back to Pennzoil and condone this conduct, or you can say, No, no, no more.

"I ask you to remember that you are in a once-in-a-lifetime situation. It won't happen again. It just won't happen. You have a chance to right a wrong, a grievous wrong, a serious wrong. It's going to take some courage. You got that. . . . You are people of morality and conscience and strength.

"Don't let this opportunity pass you."

After two hours of deliberations on Friday and six on Monday, the jurors passed two notes to Judge Casseb. One requested the definition of *wanton disregard*. The second question asked if the Texaco annual report was in evidence.

At the Texaco table, I could see their hearts sinking. It was clear that the jury had reached special issue number four, whether Pennzoil was entitled to punitive damages. The only reason they could be interested in Texaco's annual report, which was not in evidence, was to determine how much Texaco could afford to pay.

The judge defined *wanton disregard* for them and said that the annual report was not in evidence.

When we heard that the jury was ready with their verdict, I turned to Liedtke and said, "Hugh, if the answer to number one is yes, hang on, I'm going to take you for a rocket ride."

The answer to special issue number one, did they find that Pennzoil had a contract, was, "We do." That was the answer to number two, as well, that Texaco had interfered.

And when it came time for damages, the answer was "Seven point five billion dollars."

The remaining answers were all yes, and the punitive damages came to three billion dollars, for a total of ten point five. I leaned back in my chair and said to Liedtke, "Does that suit you?"

Hugh was speechless. He threw his arm around me and we hugged. The court was bedlam, packed, total bedlam. The doubters were looking at me dazed. My friends were grinning at me and giving me the closed-fist power signs. All three of our sons, Dahr, Randall, and Rob, were in the courtroom. I could see the love and pride in their eyes. I had no scarcity of friends there: Jack Crosby, Geep Hardy, Roy Cullen, and many others.

When I got home after being interviewed by the media, local, national, and international, it was about 9:00 P.M. I walked into this large room where Lee and I sometimes sit and visit with our boys, their wives, and our friends. There was a sudden burst of applause.

I looked around the room. There were Hugh and Betty Liedtke, Mildred and Baine Kerr, Lee and our sons. They were applauding me, and I felt warm all over. I kissed Lee, walked over to Betty, and said, "How do you like the jury now?"

She said, "I guess that's why I love you; you are such a good sport and a chicken shit." We drank beer and martinis and ate hamburgers. That was the extent of the celebration.

As expected, an enormous amount of maneuvering took place over the next several months. Texaco threatened bankruptcy. They succeeded in getting a New York judge to relieve them of the burden of posting a bond.

For the appeal, I asked Harry Reasoner (of Vinson & Elkins) to not just help me, but to oversee and coordinate and participate in the briefs and arguments. He did a magnificent job, as did his lawyers.

All the while, settlement talks were moving ahead. Hugh and I flew to New York and met with Carl Icahn, a big shareholder in Texaco, a smaller one in Pennzoil, who wanted to broker a deal.

I was dressed in a heavy coat, no necktie, and army boots and was in no mood to listen to any bullshit. Icahn had a young lawyer there who tried to lecture me on how we could still lose the case. I asked him, "Hey, cowboy, how many lawsuits have you tried?"

I stood and said I was leaving. "I'm done. Let's go, Hugh. I've heard all the shit I'm going to hear."

Icahn said, "Don't get mad, that won't solve anything."

I said I wasn't mad, I was just bored. He asked where I was going and I said, "To get a cold beer."

He looked startled. "It's only eleven o'clock in the morning."

I said, "Now, look, you can't be my guardian. I'm going to get a cold beer, and you're invited."

He shrugged and said, "All right, let's go."

Several people helped work out a proposal for a three-billion-dollar settlement, which was announced on December 11, 1987. It was the largest in the history of corporate America.

The next week I was back in court on another personal injury case. Don't you love happy endings?

THE
MAN WHO
CRUSHED
TEXACO

JOE JAMAIL DIDN'T WIN THE BIGGEST LAWSUIT IN THE HISTORY
OF THE WORLD BY BEING A SWEETHEART. ✪ BY JOHN DAVIDSON

(Top) Coach Darrell Royal and Willie Nelson knocked on my door, while I was writing, on the night before I was to make my closing arguments to the jury. We talked and drank until midnight. This is not the conventional way to sum up a case, but it worked out fine. (Bottom) A toast to old times not forgotten: left to right, Ronnie Krist, Geep Hardy, Jim Kronzer, Harry Reasoner, and me.

(Top) A tender moment of celebration with Hugh Liedtke, who founded Pennzoil and would not take no for an answer. (Bottom) Larry Tribe, the Harvard professor and famed constitutional lawyer (on my left), and Laurence Tisch, a Getty board member and witness for Texaco in Pennzoil v. Texaco.

The courtroom scene after the verdict: I believe this is what is called a media frenzy.

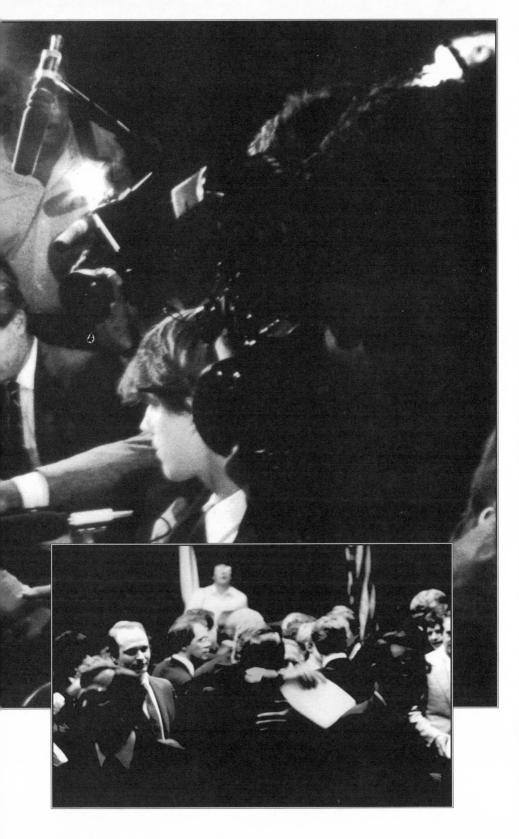

Lawyers at work: Me, Harry Reasoner, Jim Kronzer, and Hugh Liedtke, who turned his law degree into an oil company.

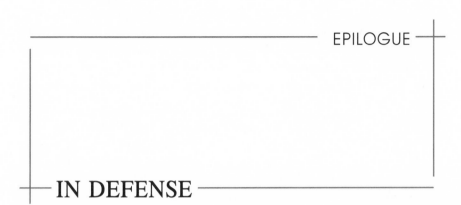

IN DEFENSE

A grave concern about the legal profession has been raised by many, including myself. The profession is viewed with distrust, dislike, and suspicion by too many people in too many places.

There is a widespread public impression that the practice of law has become primarily a money-grabbing, profit-maximizing, hustling business, rather than an admired profession. This has brought into question the intentions, integrity, and value of lawyers in general.

Lawyer bashing has become a popular indoor and outdoor sport, and lawyer jokes can be confidently relied upon to evoke loud guffaws and applause.

I believe Americans today have become the most timorous people in a very long time. The average American has forgotten the great feel for liberty and accountability that the framers of the Constitution believed in.

What the American people have today is a group of

press agents, politicians without any conviction, cheerleader types, and a manipulative media.

While I don't for a moment believe that lawyers are exclusively pure humans who have saved humanity, there are some lawyers who are worthy of the name.

I know firsthand that there are many greedy, unconcerned, dishonest attorneys in our ranks, and for that I am ashamed. They are the ones who view this as a business and not as a profession. Hell is too good for them. But I know there are those who believe in justice and equality, and they are the ones who have made a difference.

To those who decry the fact that so many people are seeking redress for wrongs through lawyers in courts, I suggest they have it all wrong. Claimants who bring their grievances to court are saying by their actions: "We are people who believe in law. We believe our court system has integrity and accessibility. The reason it has fallen to the real trial lawyers to stop the greedy, as much as we can, from grinding under the consumer and the needy is because they guard the people's rights. They take our side.

"When we seek help in the legislatures, we are powerless, for we have no money—no political action committees. And the slumbering bureaucracies of government won't respond to our pleas."

Two choices remain for the people: the courts or the streets. But direct action on the streets, in some modern form of trial by battle—we all know what horror that would bring.

These are some of the remarkable changes that trial lawyers have brought about without the aid of Congress or legislation:

• We have a government of laws, not men, thanks to lawyers.

• We have a free press, thanks to lawyers.

- We have police restrained by process, thanks to lawyers.
- We have judges and juries brave enough to seek out and pursue that eternal and best pursuit of humankind: justice.

In my time on this wrinkled prune of a planet, lawyers and judges have accomplished many sweeping improvements in the quality of justice—again, without legislation. These include:

- Desegregation of schools and much of the rest of our society.
- One man, one vote.
- Strict products liability.
- Virtual elimination of tort immunization—governmental, charitable and family.
- Rights of the retarded to education.
- The right of counsel in criminal cases.
- Rights of illegitimate children.
- The Miranda Rule—our primary protection against police state methods of interrogation and torture that are used every day in most parts of this world.
- Liability for emotional injury.
- Compensation for bereaved survivors.

The list could go on and on. I am glad to be a part of it. All these landmarks lawyers have built, and not without a purpose, not without a theme. Overall, the one great theme of law reform in our time has been equality.

Just in my lifetime, we have seen progress, mainly through the courts, in building equality. Lawyers continue to strive to build

- Equality between races,
- Equality between sexes,
- Equality between citizens and aliens,
- Equality between rich and poor,
- Equality between prosecutor and defendant.

Lawyers did this; not legislators or Congress.

From the beginning of humanity, we are told that justice is the greatest concern of man on earth. Other professions erect buildings that fall down, bridges that wash out, planes and ships that rust into obsolescence. Even the steel of a sacred symbol like our Statue of Liberty wore out in one hundred years.

Homer never built of rock or steel, nor did Socrates, nor did Jesus. They built with more enduring stuff—ideas and inspirations, beauty and truth. Likewise, lawyers build monuments with ideas and principles.

Over two centuries ago, a lawyer, Thomas Jefferson, built with ink, on paper, the Declaration of Independence. It still stands strong as a landmark of human progress, built of ideas, born of arguments, nurtured by eloquent lawyers like Patrick Henry and Samuel Adams, and, finally, made a monument on paper and etched indelibly in the minds of free men and women.

Almost as long ago, a group comprised mostly of lawyers built the Constitution, forged of the steel of arguments. Just ideas, this living Constitution. Constant building and tending by later generations of lawyers like me kept it vital and growing. Today's lawyers, including me, must constantly reinforce it.

When we talk about the law, we are talking about an organized, reasonable, accepted way for people to live together and settle their disputes without resorting to force. Everywhere we look in the world today, we see monstrous wars and atrocities, caused in large part by the absence of law as a shield for the people.

I have known people who were friendless, hopeless, poor, and despairing. I am thinking about the many times that I was called to visit the very modest home of a long-shoreman's widow and children. The men would be dressed in their suits—many of them owned only one—and their wives would be inside consoling the widow.

I had been called to help the family recover, at least,

the monetary loss they had suffered. I felt their pain and felt privileged to be with them. I could at least help restore the dignity and pride of those whose breadwinner had been negligently killed.

I am asked repeatedly why I continue to try cases. I have no answer for the questioner. But I know why. It's the memory of these sad moments, when my life became involved with the victims', that drives me.

I have been told since law school that the lawyer has to be objective, not get involved with the client emotionally. To that I say, nonsense. How can I *not* be involved? I have been involved all of my life.

Those who do not know this about me will never understand me, or how I do what I do.

I have been fortunate to help.

JOSEPH D. JAMAIL'S

SUMMATION

Pennzoil Company v. Texaco, Inc.
1985—$10.53 Billion verdict
$7.53 billion compensatory / $3 billion punitive
$11.12 billion total with interest

FOREWORD BY JAMES W. MCELHANEY

©Copyright 1992
The Professional Education Group, Inc.
12401 Minnetonka Boulevard
Minnetonka, MN 55305

Classics of the Courtroom Volume XXIV
ISBN # 0-943380-30-8

FOREWORD

November 19, 1985. Twelve jurors filed into the jury box in Harris County, Texas. The foreman handed their verdict to the bailiff, who gave it to Judge Solomon Casseb Jr. It was for $7.53 billion in compensatory damages and $3 billion in punitive damages. It was the largest verdict in the history of the United States. With interest it came to $11,120,976,110.83.

The law and the facts behind a verdict like that must be incomprehensible beyond belief, right?

Sorry. Torts and contracts still come in the first year of law school. The case was brought by Pennzoil against Texaco for the tort of interfering with Pennzoil's contract to buy Getty Oil. There was just a handful of issues: Did Pennzoil have a contract with Getty? If so, did Texaco knowingly interfere with that contract? And if Texaco interfered, what were the damages?

The story starts with the succession of power at Getty Oil, one of the nation's oil companies that was truly oil rich. Its founder, J. Paul Getty—crusty, powerful, demanding, brilliant and overbearing—wanted the reins turned over to his first-born son, George Getty II, when he stepped down.

It was a wise choice. George was dedicated and savvy and knew the oil business, but he apparently was not quite tough enough to deal with his overly exacting, bigger-than-life, domineering father. George died before his father, J. Paul, did. Apparently, he committed suicide.

Next in line was George's younger brother, Gordon Getty—a bright, flighty, unpredictable problem child and self-described "absent-minded professor." Once, J. Paul said about Gordon, "I doubt he has the qualities to make a good businessman." But in the end it was Gordon who was left in control—more or less.

After J. Paul died, Getty Oil had a board of directors

that tangled with Gordon for position. Gordon was co-trustee over the Getty family's 40 percent of the Getty Oil stock. The Getty Museum (which also jockeyed for position between Gordon and the board of directors) held an additional 12 percent of the stock. (Separate, they were minority shareholders; together, they had commanding power. Much of the negotiations in buying Getty was designed to get Gordon and the Getty Museum together or to keep them apart.)

With the most powerful family member not really disposed to running the business and the board members and stockholders angling for power, Getty Oil was no longer in the same position its founder had taken it to.

With all of its oil, it was a plum waiting to be picked—and they knew it. Getty Oil's board, Gordon, and the Getty Museum all understood that it was better to be plucked when they had some choice in the matter, rather than drop to the ground and later be picked up for a fraction of their present worth.

The two that came to fight over Getty Oil were Pennzoil and Texaco.

Pennzoil was the upstart. It began as Zapata Petroleum Company (actually named after the Marlon Brando movie *Viva Zapata!*). Zapata, by the way, was formed by Hugh Liedtke and President George H. W. Bush!

Texaco was the old player, the company that had started in 1900 and grew to be a significant force in the oil business by selling automobile gasoline. It was a marketing company that specialized in sales of consumer products. It got ahead by processing and selling other people's oil.

When Getty Oil was starting to ripen on the branch, both Pennzoil and Texaco needed oil—on and under the ground.

Pennzoil got there first. New York lawyer Arthur Liman represented Pennzoil in its attempt to buy Getty.

They went back and forth on the price, Pennzoil offering $110 a share and Getty wanting more. The price they finally settled on was $112.50 a share.

Arthur Liman said they all shook hands on the deal. David Copley, the top in-house lawyer of Getty Oil, took notes, and the *Wall Street Journal* reported an "agreement in principle."

No formal contract ever followed. Just days later, Texaco merged with Getty for $125 a share. The plum had found a more generous picker.

By the time of the trial, Getty's board denied it had ever intended to be bound by a deal with Pennzoil, Texaco denied it even knew about the deal (if, indeed, there was one) despite the article in the *Wall Street Journal,* and Getty board lawyer David Copley's notes were gone.

Pennzoil was screaming foul.

The parties were represented by two rough-and-tumble Texas trial lawyers. Pennzoil got Joe Jamail an enormously successful personal injury lawyer, who worked with a six-lawyer back-up team from Houston's Baker and Botts. Texaco got Richard Miller, the feared corporate litigator who had left Baker and Botts in 1983 to start what Miller called "my little chicken-shit law firm," Miller, Keeton, Bristow & Brown. (The word on the street in Houston was that Miller's new firm was the hottest corporate litigation outfit in town.) Jamail and Miller, by the way, were friends; Miller had actually represented Jamail just a year earlier, insisting on working for free.

Understandably, the trial was an event, with everything under the scrutiny of reporters. In the summation, Dick Miller took the gutsy step of not even arguing the defense case on damages. This was a liability case, he thought, and he did not want an argument on damages to look like a concession that Pennzoil had a contract or that Texaco had interfered with it. It was a decision that the legal news media (with the excellent clarity of hindsight) later questioned.

Joe Jamail's argument is a powerful appeal for the jury to do the right thing. Jamail intuitively knew what the recent research of Dr. Jeanne Flemming and the trial consultation firm Metricus, in Palo Alto, California, has shown—that jurors view the trial as a moral arena in which it is more important to do the right thing than to do the legally correct thing.

Listen to Jamail as he makes the jury feel responsible for setting things straight and for sending a message to Texaco. Notice how he pokes holes in the defense case and ridicules their evidence. See him deftly puncture the opposing witnesses. Then notice how it all revolves around the most powerful appeal of all—asking the jury to right a wrong.

One last word before you start on Joe Jamail's final argument. By the time the case was argued, the jury had learned a lot of names you may not know or perhaps may not be able to place in the case. Joe Jamail was talking to the jury, not to us, and he did not need to stop and explain who these people were. So before the argument is a list of some of the more important players in the case. They are listed in the order in which they appear in Jamail's summation, with just a note or two about what they did or said. Go through the list now if you like, or come back to it later if you want to check on something Joe says in his argument.

—James W. McElhaney
Case Western Reserve University
School of Law
Cleveland, Ohio
August 15, 1992

THE PLAYERS
In Order of Appearance in the Argument

(These notes are based on material drawn from Thomas Petzinger Jr.'s *Oil and Honor: The Texaco-Pennzoil Wars* [G. P. Putnam's Sons, 1987], an outstanding work of journalism by one of the rare authors who understands litigation; and John Davidson's "The Man Who Crushed Texaco," *Texas Monthly,* March 1988 p. 92, an engaging look at Joe Jamail.)

RICHARD MILLER—Texaco's lead lawyer.

HUGH LIEDTKE—Pennzoil's chairman of the board.

BLAINE P. KERR—Former partner in the Houston law firm Baker and Botts. President of Pennzoil, confidant and advisor to Pennzoil's chairman, Hugh Liedtke.

GORDON GETTY—The younger son of J. Paul Getty, who was co-trustee of 40 percent of Getty stock and who didn't want to be there in the first place.

MARTY LIPTON—Lawyer for the Getty Museum, which owned 12 percent of the Getty Oil stock. Name partner in Wachtell, Lipton, Rosen & Katz. A superstar in takeover litigation who specialized in resisting raiders, Lipton is credited with inventing the "poison pill," which protects against takeovers by letting the target company buy the raider's stock at bargain rates.

JAMES KINNEAR—Texaco's vice chairman.

LAURENCE TISCH—Getty board member who voted at the Getty meeting for the deal with Pennzoil and then testified at the trial for Texaco.

HENRY WENDT—Getty board member who voted at the Getty meeting for the deal with Pennzoil and then testified at the trial for Texaco.

CHAUNCEY MEDBERRY III—Getty board member who voted at the Getty meeting for the deal with Pennzoil and then testified at the trial for Texaco. All three—Tisch, Wendt, and Medberry—said they had never intended to be bound in an agreement with Pennzoil.

HAROLD WILLIAMS—President of the Getty Museum and former chairman of the Security Exchange Commission. The Getty Museum owned 12 percent of the Getty stock.

THOMAS BARROW—Pennzoil's damages expert, Barrow refused to accept any fee, testifying "as a matter of principle." Barrow was the vice chairman of Sohio and had an outstanding career in the field.

MARTY SIEGAL—Gordon Getty's investment banker.

GEOFFREY BOISI—Investment banker with Goldman, Sachs and Company who advised Getty Oil in its negotiations with Texaco.

SIDNEY PETERSON—Chairman of Getty Oil.

JOHN K. MCKINLEY—Chairman of Texaco.

CHARLES "TIM" COHLER—Lawyer for Gordon Getty.

BARTON WINOKUR—Lawyer for Getty Oil whom Joe Jamail calls "Back Door Bart" in his final argument.

PATRICIA VLAHAKIS—Lawyer with Wachtell, Lipton, Rosen & Katz who represented the Getty Museum.

ALFRED DeCRANE—President of Texaco who was under consideration (as was James Kinnear, the vice chairman) for chairman of Texaco.

BRUCE WASSERSTEIN—Wall Street dealmaker with First Boston Corporation.

FELIX ROHAYTN—Investment banker and boss of James Glanville.

JAMES GLANVILLE—Investment banker with Lazard Freres & Company and close friend of Pennzoil chairman Hugh Liedtke.

ARTHUR LIMAN—New York lawyer with Paul, Weiss, Rifkind, Wharton & Garrison. Liman was Pennzoil's chief negotiator on the purchase of Getty Oil.

PERRY BARBER—Former Baker and Botts lawyer who became general counsel to Pennzoil.

JOSEPH CIALONE—Merger and acquisition lawyer at Baker and Botts.

AFTERNOON SESSION
November 15, 1985

THE COURT: Y'all may take your seat.

Check the jury, please.

THE BAILIFF: Yes, sir.

THE COURT: Counsel, would y'all approach the bench for a minute?

(Whereupon, at this time, there is a discussion at the bench between the Court and counsel for both sides, the discussion being held out of the hearing of the court reporter.)

THE COURT: Bring the jury, please.

(At 1:00 P.M., the jurors are brought into the hearing of the court and the following proceedings were had:)

THE COURT: All right. Thank you.

You may be seated.

Good afternoon, ladies and gentlemen.

Court's in session.

You may proceed, Mr. Jamail.

MR. JAMAIL: Thank you, Judge Casseb.

You have listened for the last four hours for the reason for our rules of law. What lawyers tell you cannot be taken as evidence. The evidence you heard from the witness stand, from the videos, and you're going to decide the case based on what you heard.

There were so many misstatements in what Mr. Miller has told you that I'm not going to try to answer all of them. It would take all of the time.

He starts out by giving you four hours of excuses for Texaco's conduct and he ends it up by saying to you, "Don't take our company, because if something went wrong, it was Getty that did it."

They bought and paid for this lawsuit when they gave the indemnities.

They knew right then that Pennzoil had been cheated out of its agreement, but they were willing to do it, pay any cost, because to them it was cheap.

It was cheap, and we're going to get into why it was cheap.

You heard it. You heard what they saved. You know what their motive was.

And for Mr. Miller to stand here and attempt to change the Court's charge, the wording in it, by inserting things that he likes, is typical.

It's what they've done from the beginning of this case.

Judge Casseb is one of the most honored and brilliant judges in America.

If he had wanted to say to you, "contract," he would have said it. I have no quarrel with it, but it's his charge, it's not Mr. Miller's.

The reason for that is this subtle way, the attempt to try to get you, the jury, to impose a harsher burden, as he went through, the little time that he spent on the issues, for you to impose a harsher burden on Pennzoil than the law does—than the law does.

You'll—you're not going to do that. You told me when we talked the very first time—I have no reason to doubt that you're going to do what is just—you're not going to do it because I stand here and shout at you, and I hope I don't shout at you.

He's told you a lot of law—old lawyer's stories. I hope I don't take up your time doing that. I will tell you a lawyer's truism though: "When the law is on the lawyer's side, he talks about the law. When the facts are on the lawyer's side, he talks about the facts." When he has neither, he just talks—and I guess tells *Alice in Wonderland* stories.

Pennzoil's conduct is nowhere, which is above reproach. They made an open tender offer. Is that pressure?

Mr. Miller spent a great deal of time trying to attack Pennzoil through its chairman, Mr. Liedtke, and Mr. Kerr.

What did they do?

Mr. Miller, if he has his way, will introduce into the American concept of—of business a new concept, that is, Pennzoil is not allowed to purchase the Getty shares at a bargain or at a fair price to them. Now, they need to arrest everybody that goes to Foley's, then, if that's something we're going to put up with.

The reason he tells you that is because Texaco needed them and wanted those reserves; that Texaco did nothing, nothing until the time that Pennzoil and the Getty interests reached their agreement and it was announced publicly.

The timing of the tender offer is meaningless. The proof is replete. Pennzoil could not purchase any of that stock through that tender offer until January 17th. They were pressured; all they had to do was go home and that deal was over and they would have thwarted Gordon Getty again.

They said in the "Dear Hugh" letter Gordon Getty was still in a minority position.

Gordon had been treated like a nincompoop, and that's what they did. He was still in the same position with that "Dear Hugh" letter as he was in December and November and October when the Museum and Gordon Getty talked about this. Mr. Lipton told you about this, and we'll refer to it in a moment.

We got some criticism from Mr. Miller about not having our witnesses all have the very same pat story—

couldn't get their lines in the same little channel. He didn't have that trouble. Every witness they brought—reminds me of one of those squeeze dolls. You squeeze it, it says, "Free to deal. Free to deal. Free to deal." That's all we got out of them. But were they really?

In their ostrichlike hunt to find out whether or not there was an agreement between Pennzoil and the Getty interests, what did they do? What did they do? They didn't ask for the Copley notes. They know that boards of directors, when they meet, take notes, keep minutes, that Mr. Kinnear testified that getting those notes beforehand would have been diligent. That's his testimony.

Why didn't they want them? You know very well why they didn't want them. Throughout all this string of people that they brought, not one of them told you that they asked for the Copley notes or that they asked what the board voted on.

Now, Mr. Miller has told you, and it's right, that you can't take testimony after the fact and make it apply to this case. What was in the intent or in the minds of those parties at the time is what the case needs to be decided on, and you're admonished to do that.

And yet, every witness that he relied on, Mr.—from that board of directors, Mr. Tisch, Mr. Wendt, and Mr. Medberry—are after-the-fact witnesses. "Well, we didn't intend"—but what is the proof? What is the proof? You know what the proof is.

The proof is the memorandum of agreement. It doesn't say anything about having to be signed by the company, it says approved by the company. Approved.

It was signed and what in—what you must ask yourselves, the company's only objective was price. They were gone. The rest of this was between Gordon Getty and the Trust and Pennzoil. It was up to them to make the determination, the future course.

So, the price was obviously discussed by that board

and you go back to the—to the testimony, there's a record of it, there's an exhibit in this testimony, on December the 30th or 31st, the museum and the company and Gordon Getty, I think this is Mr. Lipton's testimony, agreed that $110, they were sellers.

And what happened? Now, the company, in its war—ongoing war with Gordon Getty—had one thing in mind, obviously—the old directors, that is—to prevent Gordon Getty from fulfilling the wishes of the Trust, his family, his father, and himself, and that is to regain control of that company, and they were at war with him.

They made a decision on their own that Gordon's father didn't know what he was talking about when he wanted it to stay in the family. He was dead, he couldn't defend himself. So, the "Dear Hugh" letter gave Gordon Getty no more authority than he had months before.

Incensed about it? Mr. Lipton told you, he testified—I think I have it here—that he knew the context of it on January the 1st. He told Mr. Williams before the board meeting. It didn't outrage him.

And if it so outraged that board of directors, it was done, you know, on the—on the late evening or early morning of January 2nd.

They recessed, went home, thought about it, came back, and went on to make their counterproposal on price and approved the Pennzoil plan.

Now, Mr. Miller made something about the indemnities that were presented to Mr. Liedtke by the museum and the company. Those were all to the standstill agreement. That wouldn't alert anybody, that was things that they had done among themselves.

There is a major difference in the indemnity that Texaco gave to the Getty interests, and I want to talk to you about those again in a moment.

Now, you heard from Mr. Miller so many misstatements. Let me correct one of them now. He stood here and, in a plea for sympathy, which you are admonished in Judge Casseb's instructions to you not—not to let influence you, "That we only have $10 billion in our company."

That's not so. The assets of Texaco are in excess of $48 billion. That's what their assets are.

He tells you that Mr. Barrow's testimony is—should be tainted for some reason. What? He came here without pay because, as he put it, "An important principle is at stake here."

And make no mistake about it, it is.

He said that Mr. Kerr was on the board of directors at American General Insurance with Mr. Barrow.

That is false. Mr. Kerr is not now, never has been on that board, and was never asked to be on that board. Why he would try to tell you that is beyond me, except it's the "win at any cost" philosophy of Texaco. Because "Even if we lose here, we've won. We got Getty and you can't take that away from us."

So, that remedy that the law provides for us is to be here before you, but don't make any mistake about it, they don't want this. That's our remedy. And they ask—you know, you don't see Getty in here, you don't see the museum in here, you don't see the trust in here. For what purpose?

For what purpose, jury?

After they've guaranteed them and protected them from this very contingency, Pennzoil's lawsuit.

Well, why would there be any question in having them here, or for what reason?

And, I asked you this when we first talked and tried to explain it to you then, and all of you told me at that time that—if that—if that came down that way, that was fine, you could find on the facts you heard.

But that's another smoke screen.

Anybody but Texaco, anybody but Texaco, and listen,

our fallback position at Texaco is this: "This is a revenge case. This is frivolous."

I don't believe that that should be dignified by any answer.

I will make a statement, however, that if that were so, do you think that Judge Farris in a year and a half, and Judge Casseb lately, would have allowed us to progress this far?

No. We have met every test the law has provided. Every one.

The law says, "Go."

And now it's up to you.

Another smoke screen? I don't know—well, I don't want to talk about that.

It's fairly insulting, as I see it, after four and a half months, to call this some sort of revenge case when they deliberately stand before you and distort, misrepresent, the evidence.

You can read it.

He says to you, "We weren't alone. Excuse us. Excuse us. There was Socal bidding. There was Mobil bidding and there was the Saudi government bidding," the old Saudi connection that Texaco has.

And you heard that testimony Mr. McKinley volunteered.

But the problem they've got with this is nobody followed through but Texaco. Nobody. Everybody backed off.

And you remember Gordon Getty's testimony when he talked to the Saudi government on January the 4th.

Mr. Yamani or Mr. Shaheen, and the words were, "It's a done deal."

Did Gordon Getty think he had a binding agreement? Did he? Did he think he had an agreement with Pennzoil when he said to those people, "It's a done deal," when he sends Mr. Siegal's affidavit, with his approval, to

California to tell that court, "Transaction now agreed upon"?

I really don't want you to—don't believe that affidavit. You know lawyers make those things up. He embraces Mr. Siegal part of the time and denounces him at other times.

Can he have it both ways?

We have nothing to gain from Mr. Siegal saying that. But in his testimony, his deposition, Mr. Siegal testified by deposition that what he said in that affidavit on January the 5th was true and correct then.

Those are his words. What changed?

The higher price, the indemnities, the limited warranties. And Texaco, still continuing its very selective investigation of the facts, says, well, listen jury, if you don't believe that, we talked to all these people, all these people, Mr. Boisi, Mr. Petersen, to Mr. Lipton, these people.

And they told us free to deal, free to deal. Free to deal. And, oh, by the way, they all stood to make millions on it if we upped this price and they—but they gave us their word, free to deal.

That's good enough for Mr. McKinley, who, from his testimony, recognizes no good faith dealings, only fair, not good faith.

The judge asked you about good faith, and finally they say these people who have these millions to make on this deal told us okay to deal.

But when it came time for those very people to put in writing the words they had been telling these folks, or they said they've been telling them, they balked.

They wouldn't do it.

As a matter of fact, they did the reverse. They said no. Now, listen, we told you this and we really—we really mean it, but when you get it down to put it in writing and in this agreement between Texaco and the Getty entities, we're going to have to have these indemnities.

Does that sound like free to deal?

And the specific indemnity against any claim of any kind against you made by Pennzoil. Does that sound like free to deal?

Wouldn't that alert somebody? And in addition to that, we're going to require on behalf of the museum and on behalf of the trust that you take this stock with this reservation on it.

We own it except we make no reservation as to Pennzoil's ownership of this stock.

Wouldn't that alert somebody? Well, it would me. And it should have them, and it did Mr. McKinley, and I'll come to that in a few minutes because he testified that that would alert but yet that's exactly how they took it. It's exactly how they took that stock.

The guaranteed price of $112.50, is that a coincidence?

No. The museum knew and understood that it had a firm deal with Pennzoil at that price. They were not going to let that bird get out of hand.

They knew that they could then deal with impunities if they got the indemnity and the limited warranty and they could keep what they had by forcing Texaco if anything went wrong to guarantee $112.50.

Now, we didn't—that didn't come out of my *Alice in Wonderland*. That came to you from this witness stand and from these documents.

What do you do with that? What do you do with that? Is that knowingly avoiding and intentionally avoiding finding out what went on?

Well, you are saying this to me but you won't write it down. I think maybe you ought to look at your board minutes and see what was voted on on January 2nd and 3rd. Didn't do any of that and listen, by the way, did anybody file any papers anywhere that would shed some light on this?

Anybody saying that there is an agreement, that you really aren't free to deal?

Nobody asked any of those questions.

And they're in the very same room in the Pierre Hotel with Gordon Getty and his wife and Mr. Siegal, standing there, and just hours before Mr. Siegal had filed the affidavit in California saying that there was a—an agreed transaction.

And what do they do with Mr. Cohler's testimony? Foolishly, they get him to go back and try to change a couple of hours later. What are they covering up?

And the Copley notes? The third edition of the Copley notes? I'm glad they're here. I'm glad they're here.

Page 63, which they want to gloss over, tells us a story about what was voted on by that board. But you may, and you are entitled to ask yourselves, "I wonder what those originals looked like before they went to work on them in those Dechert-Price law firm, the offices? I wonder what they looked like. I wonder if they're just even, not more favorable to Pennzoil's position?"

And he stands there and wants to tell you that Pennzoil destroyed some records, pieces of paper in which they had "what ifs."

You had all that "what if" for days here, public stuff that came out of public records, not board minutes.

And there was no lawsuit and none anticipated before any tender offer was made.

But what did Getty do after Texaco took them?

Mr. Copley goes to the Texaco offices and meets with some of the executives there and I suppose the first official act he did when he got back to his offices was to go over to the Dechert-Price offices, Mr. Winokur's law firm, and destroyed them after editing them.

Why did he have to go to White Plains and then come back and do that? You're entitled to ask yourselves these kinds of questions.

And I wonder what they truly would have shown but they couldn't get enough out of there because on page 63 when Mr. Williams asked Mr. Lipton or Mr. Petersen, the chairman, excuse me, Mr. Petersen asked Mr. Lipton to restate the proposal, he talks about the structure of the company.

You've read it. You don't need me to tell you about it again. It's there. It's there.

With the counterproposal made by Getty, they were accepting the Pennzoil plan, which was the only plan before them.

It's referred to as the Pennzoil proposal.

What else can they do?

Mr. Lipton from that witness stand said to you that if they had meant price, they would have said price approved, as to price only.

I'm going to read this. I've got the line and pages. That's what he said. They didn't say that.

Now, after the fact, which testimony that we have agreed is not evidence from which you should consider the answer to these issues, after the fact, we hear about price only.

If Mr. Lipton did not believe that he had a bound agreement with Pennzoil, why, when the self-tender came up in the Copley notes, was he insisting on that $115 guarantee price from the company?

It's in the record.

And they fall back on that old line of defense, fiduciary relationship.

Well, I want to talk to you about fiduciary relationship for a moment. The judge instructs you as to that, and there's testimony in the case that you have heard that says there's a time when that relationship ends, once you make an agreement, then that's it.

The fiduciary, no matter what he is, cannot by himself or herself go out and say, "All right. I made this agreement with you but now I'm not going to live up to it. King's X."

And he can't say, "I never really secretly in my heart intended to keep it."

That's part of the defense. I want to talk to you about it.

I suppose when Texaco talks to you about good faith and fiduciary, we have to start with, with the Getty board's lawyer that has adopted the Texaco position and their witnesses that came on their behalf and they admitted to you—Ms. Vlahakis's deposition, she told you and the rest of them because of the full and complete indemnities that were given by Texaco, it was incumbent upon them and necessary that they have to come and, and testify.

But to help them defend the case, which she was helping them do.

They spent a lot of time by their own admission with these witnesses.

They had no choice but to come and give you some suggestive after-the-fact opinion. That's what they did.

That's what they did. But I suppose we have to start with Mr. Bart Winokur and Mr. Boisi back in Houston. You say what has that got to do with it. Well, it has some idea of how Texaco views fiduciary relationship and good faith because they have adopted and they vouched for him when they put him on. You remember him, backdoor Bart? Snuck in the back door when they got Gordon Getty out of the room? Kicked him off or tried to instigate a lawsuit to kick him off the board of trust of his own family trust?

Instigated, funded a lawsuit to remove or in the alternative to appoint a co-trustee who could dominate him.

That's really good faith and that's a lot of fiduciary.

They really laid a whole lot of fiduciary on Gordon Getty, and that's what you are dealing with, and he stands here and wants to talk about morality?

Not today.

And anyway, he says how can you expect us to know about something that's in the January 4th *Wall Street Journal* or in the—on the broad tape, or whatever it is.

That's the one day in history that nobody in Texaco saw or read the *Wall Street Journal*. And there's a—they swear to that.

(At this time there is loud commotion in the court-room.)

THE COURT: Order in the court.

MR. JAMAIL: They swear to that with an interrogatory.

We asked them: It's not fair to ask them in May under oath. What's unfair about that?

If you have somebody that saw it, come tell us. And if that's not important to them, why do they deny having seen it?

You are entitled to ask yourselves that. Why that big denial, under oath? They didn't—they didn't see it. They didn't see it because they didn't want to see it.

And they—the excuse or alibi regarding the indemnity, now, that was a strong excuse. It came from Mr. DeCrane, I believe. He said that Mr. Williams's paranoia affected his psyche so terrible that he needed this indemnity for peace of mind.

But Mr. Williams never said that, and Mr. Lipton never said that.

Do you suppose that Gordon Getty needed it for his peace of mind?

Is that why they gave him this? Do you suppose that all of the agents and representatives that Texaco indemnified for the museum and the trust needed it for their psyche and their peace of mind?

Do you suppose that the Getty board of directors were so paranoid that their psyches needed easing through the indemnity so they could rest easy? It was to make them rest easy, but it wasn't because of any psyche.

They know and knew at that moment that those indemnities came up, hey, there's a problem here.

But the problem is not as big as the one we've got over here, which is depleting assets, the reserves.

And listen, we're going to do all of this, we at Texaco, and we're going to do it because it's fair. We're going to do it because it's competition.

We're going to go and raise the price. We're going to give indemnities. We're going to give these warranties.

We're going to guarantee the price of the museum because that's competition and that's fair.

And it's fair if we do it in secret. That's what's really fair about it.

Well, you might ask yourselves, well, why wouldn't you just call—you wanted to talk to the people who were involved in this—why wouldn't you just call somebody at Pennzoil and ask them?

Oh, they can't do that. That would be too fair. You just can't be—you can't do that. We did it and Mr. McKinley testified and Mr. Kinnear intentionally and knowingly and the testimony is—and I have it scribbled out here and the page number—that Mr. McKinley knows of no other reason why the Pennzoil-Getty transaction was not finalized, formalized, knows of no other reason except Texaco's conduct.

And neither did Mr. Lipton, and you know right now that if Texaco had not done what they had done and these parties were left to their own devices, that on January 3rd that agreement would have been fulfilled and formalized and we wouldn't be here today.

There were no other bidders. The public had known about this strife and this company for months. The stock had hovered somewhere between $45 and $40, whatever it was.

Stealing the company and going in and offering $112.50, 40 percent more than the stock was selling for in the market—how is that hurting the public shareholders? I don't know. I don't know. The—

I want to talk with you now about the friendly Texaco, if I may. They paint this picture of this great big friendly teddy bear that has these law offices and law firms represent them everywhere and they have one that they've used for years in New York. But when it came down to the time for this acquisition, did they call them? Nope.

Why not? Well, we called Skadden-Arps. They are the biggest takeover lawyers in the country, right ahead of Lipton's group—office a couple of blocks from each other—and why did they hire Skadden-Arps? Why didn't they go to their people?

As you remember, Mr. Wasserstein's conversation or Boisi's on the 4th with Lipton, Lipton suggested that they hire Skadden-Arps, Mr. Lipton, the lawyer for the museum, the lawyer for Mr. Tisch, and the lawyer for Mr. McKinley and Texaco.

He was the engineer. And they got to him and they stopped the train. It's just that simple, and they did it, and he slicked them with impunities.

He got his price, got his floor and the warranties he specially set and the indemnities. And you might ask yourselves—they try to explain this warranty thing, that the reason for that is we didn't want to violate the indemnity clause and that's the reason we—that you see in here this limited warranty.

Well, that ought to tell us something, shouldn't it? That the only way that the indemnity could be voided is if Getty or the museum or the trust misrepresented something.

Now, think about it.

So if they had not limited that warranty on the stock by saying we don't make any claim as against Pennzoil if that had not been in there, then the indemnity that Texaco gave them, Texaco could have kicked out the window because they would have said you didn't tell us about this claim that Pennzoil got on your stock.

And that's the reason.

It's a fatal flaw in their argument and it's telling you, it's compelling evidence that they wanted—the museum and these other parties wanted so much to guard these indemnities that they disclosed to them, that we're not telling you we own this stock free and clear as it affects Pennzoil.

Does that tell us something? They even admitted it that it was relative to the indemnity. No explanation for that from them.

They said, well, we've got this great big open point, employee benefits.

Pennzoil doesn't even address that. Of course not. Pennzoil was going in on a different basis than Texaco. Pennzoil was going to be a minority, three-sevenths owner or partner, if you please, with the—with the Getty Trust, which would have conformed with the provisions of that trust. Texaco was to take the entire company.

That was their—as they told you—that was their motive, their plan and the strategy, the rest of it. But that isn't what the resolution said.

It gives them some leverage to squeeze on Gordon because it authorized them to buy a majority of the shares, not all the shares.

They said, well, that isn't what the intent was. You know we're dealing with people who supposedly know how to read and write.

And you have to take them at their word at that time, not their alibis later in the courtroom.

The last thing they wanted was to be in Texas before a Texas jury, but the law provided that, and that's why we're here.

They say these employee benefits, Pennzoil callously disregarded it.

That wasn't going to change. They would have you believe that these employees were going to be without any pension plans or anything else.

Their pension plan, one of the best in the country until they got it dismantled when Texaco took them, the pension plan was in effect, would have stayed in effect.

There was no cancellation of that. That's a rabbit trail. That is the octopus defense. It's to spew ink everywhere to confuse and confound when you don't have the facts.

You look at it.

The testimony in this case from Mr. Liedtke and Mr. Kerr, that plan would have remained in effect, taking care of those employees because we at Pennzoil did not intend nor could we terminate these people. We needed them to run the company.

We had to have them but let's—so that's the reason. There didn't have to be one. Later when it came up that it was using the Pennzoil employment plan, was taken by the Getty lawyers and stuck into the Texaco agreement, the proposal that they had later worked on on the 4th, but it was not necessary to Pennzoil to address that problem.

If there was going to be some problem about this agreement, why was Gordon Getty trying to persuade Mr. Hugh Liedtke to go to California with him to talk to the employees on the next day to assure them?

There's objective evidence of this contract. I want to get back into it with you, but I'll say this. Texaco really did take care of those employees.

They really did. Wholesale firing, paying them with their own money out of their pension and employment benefits and trying to get you to believe that they did something.

And then when Mr. McKinley testified, other than the golden parachutes to the twelve executives who were instrumental in trying to get this Pennzoil deal undone and their deal done, those nine—excuse me—executives got over $12 million plus their stock options, and I think he testified the employees had been paid $78 million, so they must have fired a lot more since then because there's $4 million now four months later.

But then he says in answer to a question that I asked him that yes, Texaco did in fact attempt to and planned to take $250 million in cash out of that employees' benefit and retirement fund.

For what purpose, Mr. McKinley?

Well, to—office expenses and run the—run the shop. They really treated them fair. They got $250 million, leave them the piece of paper, IOU or something.

That's neat. That is really looking out after employees that you are going to fire, which is what they did.

So, I tell you this only because it was not any open point between the Getty entities and Pennzoil, because they knew that Pennzoil was not going to be firing employees, that the Getty plan would remain in effect and Pennzoil was a minority stockholder.

The situation changed when Texaco came in.

It would then be, perhaps, but not with Pennzoil. Because that's an after-the-fact thought, another rabbit trail for you.

Anything they can do, anything except the facts, pressure. Okay. They say finally pressure made us do it.

Only Mr. Medberry had enough courage to stand up to the pressure.

Well, that got out, and then it comes back and says, no, Mr. Lipton says Mr. Medberry is just a strange case. You wouldn't really understand.

I guess I don't.

But if that thing was meaningless, that Pennzoil proposal, and the board approval of it was meaningless, is Mr. Medberry just some stubborn old coot that by golly he's not going to vote yes to anything? What's the purpose? What's the purpose?

Mr. Lipton on pressure, when I asked him the question, page 17760 in the transcript, for the record.

I know you don't have that in your head.

"The pressure by Pennzoil was not what motivated the board to vote 15 to 1 on the counterproposal they made."

I'm quoting it.

"The pressure that was motivating the board went beyond the Pennzoil tender offer and was caused by two major shareholders who had previously acted by consent combined with the proposal to acquire the company at $110 when Getty's investment banker was stating that it was an inadequate price."

Now, that's his testimony,

The pressure was put on by he, Lipton.

The "Dear Hugh" letter did not shock him, that he had discussed it. Page 17791, that he had discussed it with Mr. Williams prior to this meeting.

It was the very same concept that he had discussed with the same people in October of that year. He had described. They say this came as a bombshell. He, Lipton, described the "Dear Hugh" letter to Mr. Williams, the president of that board of directors and the museum, the day before the board meeting. At least Mr. Williams knew about it. He discussed it with the board.

And along that line of questioning I thought it was really strange Mr. Lipton blurted out something about an agreement, a binding agreement. And I think it's worth looking at.

"There's a different standard in my mind between ordinary people making contracts with each other and whether or not it's a $10 billion deal."

To him money is the object. That's what it is. That's what he said.

That this could be construed—it could be an agreement.

He says this Pennzoil thing. People can agree without lawyers, but in his mind the amount of money makes the difference.

And that's that specialized group you had to deal with that would have injected themselves into our business community and into our law, calling themselves mergers and acquisitions lawyers, carving up corporate America to their liking and nobody loses. Those investment bankers and the lawyers that comprise this mergers and acquisitions field, they get together. They're all within a couple of miles of each other. One wins one day and another wins another day, and the investment bankers win all the days and they win with these indemnities.

Do you think for a minute that Marty Lipton or that Mr. Siegal, the adviser, or Woodhouse for the trust would have for one minute, one minute agreed to this Texaco deal without those indemnities?

I know you've heard the testimony. Mr. McKinley says it was an essential part. And you heard Lipton on it. Mr. Lipton about Mr. Williams and pressure, page 17830 of the transcript.

Lipton assured us that Williams always honored his signature. Well, it's on the memorandum of agreement.

I quote: "Williams had no pressure applied to him by Pennzoil when he signed the memorandum of agreement."

That's Mr. Lipton. That's Williams's lawyer.

How do they get it standing here before you telling you about all this terrible pressure when here's a man testifying to you that there wasn't any Pennzoil pressure? He applied it. Then later came on to say: "Well, maybe. But the real pressure was me, Marty Lipton, because we were the swing." 17879 of the transcript. Lipton testifying.

"No one had a gun at Williams's head or forced him to make the motion to the board to adopt the Pennzoil proposal."

"Gun at the head" is another slogan they've invented.

Kind of like "free to deal." Kind of like that and kind of like other things.

Pressure. Gordon Getty's testimony in this record:

QUESTION: "Can you recall your conversation with Siegal while he was still in the Virgin Islands?"

ANSWER: "Yes, I can recall a conversation or two with him."

QUESTION: "Can you recall what the two of you said?"

ANSWER: "Well, once again we remembered odd things. But I remembered this. He thought that the Pennzoil tender was a very helpful and promising development."

That's Gordon Getty's sworn testimony. He did not see it as they did. He saw it as an opportunity.

QUESTION: "And what did you understand him to mean by that?"

ANSWER: "I didn't ask him."

QUESTION: "Did you agree with him?"

ANSWER: "Certainly."

QUESTION: "Why did you view it as an opportunity?"

ANSWER: "Well, one step raised the price of the stock quite a bit. That's what I was trying to do."

Is that threatened by the tender offer? You've got the two major parties who signed the agreement. It was not necessary that the board sign it. You read it. I'm not going to take up your time. It says: "With approval of the board." It becomes a binding—it becomes effective.

And you trace it. You trace it through the—you trace it through the Copley notes on 63. You trace it through the Garber notes, which is really—you know, this is Mr. Copley.

And Mr. Lipton testified that Copley would know as to whether the board bound itself to an agreement.

This is Mr. Copley talking to Mr. Garber, the treasurer of Texaco. This is an agreement.

"Trust, museum plus Pennzoil. Board agreed, but for Chauncey"—Medberry—"the deal should be done."

You know, that's plain. There's nothing complicated about that.

"Pennzoil to purchase," and it goes on. "Getty to buy other shares, less shares owned by Pennzoil in a cash-out merger. Pennzoil to take museum."

I don't know what else you do when the secretary and the top lawyer for Getty is telling his treasurer, who needs to know on the West Coast, and the treasurer takes these notes.

"Board voted deal should be done."

And they're not talking about prices only. They're talking about who's buying shares and other things, how it's going to be done.

And you don't need to just rely on that. You can go to the memorandum of agreement, 63, the press release and the notes. And they all conform. They all conform.

Judge Casseb asks you in the charge, and we need the first instruction that you get, by the way, is one we talked about at length, if you remember, when we were questioning you earlier in the voir dire about the measure of proof and I had told you then that having dealt with Texaco and its lawyers for the year and a half in this case prior to getting here, that I felt that it was not going to be possible for me to extract a confession on the stand Perry Mason-like from these people, that in fact they did knowingly interfere with Pennzoil's contract, and that the law did not require that of me or Pennzoil.

And you all agreed that the standard was a reasonable one, and that was preponderance of the evidence. And I know—I've looked at some of you during that and you got tired of me asking you about it.

I told you and defined it the best I could and told you if you could picture in your mind's eye the scale of justice and if it tipped in one direction then that's all the law requires. Less than 51 percent.

It's not a rule I made up. It's been ingrained in our law since we have been a country and it's one that we are sworn to follow. Not beyond a reasonable doubt.

So I ask you to pay—I think that the evidence is overwhelming. You know whether these people had a meeting of the minds on that day. Not what somebody comes and excuses in alibis and tries to explain away.

The—you told me then that that's the measure of proof—the standard of proof that you would follow?

And that's the one that Judge Casseb admonishes you that we must follow, and it means the greater weight and degree of credible evidence.

Now, you turn to special issue number one, and you can read it as well as I can.

"Do you find," from the test that we just spoke about, "from a preponderance of the evidence that at the end of the Getty Oil board meeting on January 3rd," at that moment, not later, "that these Getty entities and Pennzoil intended to bind themselves to an agreement that included the following terms."

An agreement. And again, if Judge Casseb wanted to say written contract, he knows how to do that. He didn't. The law requires no such harsh burden of us. Would be impossible.

And you see and you go back to the Copley notes, and you go back to the press release, and you go back to the memorandum of agreement, and you go back to the Garber notes, and you go to the January 5th newspaper release in which it confirms that an agreement had been reached, the turmoil is over.

And it talks about an agreement no less than fifteen times. What can we do? What more can we bring you?

Well, there was one other thing. Mr. Petersen, brilliant one moment, experienced one moment, and not knowing what he's saying the next moment after the *Fortune* magazine article appeared. He just didn't know what he was saying when he said, "We approved the Pennzoil deal but we didn't like it. We approved it because it was a bird-in-the-handish situation."

What did that mean? Mr. McKinley doesn't know. He doesn't know. Perhaps by your verdict you can tell him. Everybody else knew. Mr. Tisch knew. "It means the same to everybody," Mr. Tisch says.

"Everybody knows what that means. We didn't have anything else. We didn't like it. They didn't like it because Gordon Getty was finally going to get to have some control over his family's company. But we approved it."

You know, we didn't give that interview. It's unrefuted. Uncorrected. He didn't do anything. There it is glaring at us. You know, we didn't have a gun at Mr. Petersen's head when he told those people at *Fortune* magazine what he told them.

And they ask you to ignore that. They ask you to ignore all of this compelling evidence, much as they ignored Pennzoil's rights the same way. As they ignored asking for any information that would give them concrete evidence as to whether or not these people were fair to deal—free to deal.

They avoided it like the plague. They knew it was there. They knew those notes were there. They knew the indemnities were there.

I have no way—other than what I have spent my time trying to talk to you about—to tell you any more about what these people intended. It's not what Texaco tells you they intended. The judge doesn't say that to you. He tells you that it's what those parties intended, not subject to Texaco's interpretation.

I believe under all this evidence it would be disastrous if special issue number one were answered any way except "We do. We do."

It doesn't ask you about employees' rights. It doesn't ask you about whether it's going to be a merger. It doesn't ask you whether or not all of those smoke screens Texaco has brought to you.

It asks you about these three things: the price, the three-sevenths/four-sevenths, which was Getty's idea. The number he and Mr. Siegal took credit for. That's what they wanted. And then the third one in case they could not agree—which nobody has told you was an unreasonable provision. In case they could not agree they would split it up and go their own way.

They're not giving Pennzoil anything. Pennzoil has paid billions of dollars for this privilege. And if Pennzoil didn't think it had a deal, why did it transfer or make arrangements to transfer a billion dollars in cash overnight so the museum shares could be put in escrow?

That's what Mr. Miller was insisting on telling you that we didn't have any expenses incurred in that transfer of money. But nonetheless it was partial performance of that agreement.

Why would we be doing that?

Evidence, my friends. That's what we decide cases in this country on, not what lawyers tell you they think you ought to do, how they think you should interpret what they want you to interpret. What you've seen. What you've heard. The instructions are important.

You go back to Mr. DeCrane's notes where he says oral argument—only an oral agreement. Excuse me. Only an oral agreement.

Well, the judge tells you you can have an oral agreement. That's our law. It's been ingrained in our law. Otherwise, you couldn't deal. You don't need a lawyer there and a stenographer taking down what you're doing with somebody. That happens afterwards.

As Mr. McKinley said in his testimony about the definitive merger agreement, it's what the lawyers do, the detail after the executives agree.

And that's in the testimony.

Now, does the press release say anything about subject to board approval? Nowhere. And they know how to do this.

You remember when I had Mr. Lipton on the stand I presented these things, the other mergers he's been in. Everyone that wanted to say board approval said that.

The judge is not asking you about that. He's asking you did they agree on these items, and then he instructs you about these items. You need to go to the intent.

And one important thing about number two, if there's any sanity, dignity, and morality left in the business community, one provision is that you cannot deal with me and harbor in your heart some secret that you're going to turn around and stick a knife in me, which is what they claim they did.

"Well, we never told Pennzoil that we didn't intend to be bound, but the board secretly had in mind shopping the deal."

Judge Casseb says you can't do that. If that's their defense, we've got a binding agreement on these points. You can read it. You can read it.

This Question No. 1 is not determined by the parties, secret, inward or subjective intentions. Can't do that. There's no requirement that a more formal and detailed document be signed. That's not my law. I didn't make that up. It's our law. Yours. Mine. The Court gives this law to us. That you agree and then later on you may sign all these formal instruments. And that's binding. And that's binding.

And we're bound to follow these instructions. Even if there were other matters left for future negotiations, Your Honor tells you that would not defeat a binding agreement.

Cannot because you never would have one then. That's Instruction No. 4.

No. 5 carries that age-old concept of our law that we must deal with ourselves and each other in good faith.

Was it good faith to pull Ms. Vlahakis away from the meeting when they were finalizing the formal agreement? Is that good faith? Was it good faith to mislead Pennzoil and keep them on the hook and then one by one call away the Getty lawyers with Texaco's knowledge?

They're in Lipton's office. And they're calling them over to Lipton's office. One by one calling them away from there so they could not finalize it. Is that good faith? They're obligated.

Every binding agreement carries with it a duty of good faith. If these people intended to be bound, that good faith requirement obviously has not been lived up to.

Now, you say, well, you know they got this memorandum of agreement and the Pennzoil proposal but the board rejected it on the first vote and now we've got this counterproposal but it goes back on page 63 to the wording of the memorandum of agreement. You say, well, it's not the very same now as the memorandum of agreement because the price has changed from $110 to $110 plus the stub.

Well, that's the reason in our law that we have things such as—that allow people who intend to be bound to modify things in that binding agreement.

His Honor tells you in Instruction No. 6: "The modification or discussions to modify an agreement may not defeat or nullify a prior intention to be bound."

Now, they didn't address this with you. They only told you, well, it's changed. But the judge has instructed you that that kind of modification does not defeat the agreement.

Now, what objective evidence is there of this contract? Of course, I've told you the memorandum of agreement with the museum, the trust, the letter from Gordon Getty to Mr. Liedtke, the "Dear Hugh" letter. And then very importantly on the fourth—excuse me—the fourth objective item. On January 3rd the letter that Mr. Hugh Liedtke wrote to the board telling them that this was a modification as to price only. And some of—Mr. Tisch said he never saw it or didn't remember seeing it.

But the unequivocal proof from Mr. Lipton is that it was delivered and that he saw it and Mr. Williams saw it in the boardroom.

Obviously, Mr. Liedtke and the board—Mr. Liedtke knew and the board knew that the only thing that Mr. Liedtke was willing to modify was the price. Other terms were intact. And that exhibit is in evidence and you've seen it and it's the letter to the board spelling out one of the prior counterproposals from the board that he would modify as to price.

There's the press release by the Getty Oil Company as objective evidence, and the other Getty entities. There's the press release by Pennzoil as objective evidence. It just tracks the Getty press release.

There's the January *Wall Street Journal* news article.

There's a Getty corporate employees' newsletter sent out January 4th assuring and trying to ease any fears the employees may have had.

I think evidence of a binding agreement is the destruction of the Copley notes even with the edited version. It forces only one conclusion, and that is there was a binding agreement.

There's the *Fortune* magazine article.

There's the Siegal affidavit.

There's the Copley notes.

There's the Cohler affidavit.

There's the Garber notes.

There's the DeCrane and Lynch notes.

Now, there's something else. There's that bill that's in

evidence from those bankers, investment bankers, Goldman-Sachs—Mr. Boisi's outfit—dated January 4th. The bill to the Getty Oil Company for their services. Six million dollars, I think it was.

Do you remember Mr. Tisch testifying? Well, I've got it somewhere. Page 20405 of his transcribed sworn testimony answering about Goldman-Sachs sending that fee bill to the Getty Oil company on January 4th.

He acknowledged, "That such fee statements are usually not sent until a transaction is binding and complete." That's Mr. Tisch.

Did he have a gun at his head when he swore to that? Objective evidence. I don't know what else we can do.

We had to take the things they had and come to you because, even the edited things—because they did it secretly—and come to you and show you what happened to Pennzoil that had dealt openly and in good faith by making its public tender offer.

If Texaco really wanted to bid fairly and complete, nothing prevented them from going out and making a tender offer for $120, $125. Pennzoil could be no threat at $100. Who is going to send in their stock to Pennzoil at that price?

That's the way you compete. You don't compete by doing, as Mr. DeCrane's notes tell, "Create concern of economic loss to Gordon Getty. The problem is we can't get Gordon Getty on base first so let's manufacture some real work for Gordon after smearing him with that fiduciary stuff we did in Houston. Let's do some of that to him."

That's Texaco morality. And they did create it. And they say it's an accident when it says in these notes, "that the ideal way to consummate this is to get the museum first. Marty Lipton the key." That doesn't mean anything. I don't want you to think about that, jury, because if you do you might have some independent thoughts that don't coincide with Texaco's wishes.

Really commands. Mr. Miller told you you couldn't find a contract.

I tell you, I plead with you that under the evidence you should. That's all I can do. So that doesn't mean anything. Means nothing.

This stop the train, stop the signing, we've got Mr. McKinley's admission. "I told him I hope you don't sign this until you hear my offer." This is Mr. Lipton talking to his lawyer—Mr. McKinley talking to his one-time lawyer, Mr. Lipton.

Did they follow that script at that strategy meeting? He stopped the signing. But he did nicely.

He says, "I hope you won't sign anything until you consider my substantially higher offer." I guess that's called nice—stop the signing. Stop the train. They didn't stop it. They derailed it, blew it up.

Well, they stopped the signing and they got to Lipton. First, when they went to see and they got the museum shares locked up, if you believe Mr. Williams before they went to the Pierre, who said that Lipton had called him, told him he had a deal for $125 a share.

You know, this didn't come out of *Alice in Wonderland*. It came from right here. They don't want you to accept it that way because, you see, jury, the way they've got it figured you shouldn't look at the clear evidence.

Don't believe what you see. Don't believe what you hear. We know best. We know best. Believe what we tell you, and then America will be strong.

That's really wonderful. I just don't think it will happen that way.

So they did, they got over there and Mr. DeCrane says there wasn't any real intent about all this.

I just jotted this stuff down at this strategy meeting. It was just an accident, I guess, that the Museum shares fell first.

And then they wanted to deny to you that they pressured Gordon Getty.

But what does Gordon Getty have to say about it?

Gordon Getty told you in his videotape, the last thing he said to you was, among the last things, was—and would have told you this—the clear—that Marty Lipton left no doubt that the museum was selling.

Where would that leave Gordon Getty? Except then in a minority position with a one-company owner, Texaco, at their total mercy.

At that point, squeezed out, leaving him with paper.

Now they can't explain their own notes.

They used the words. They didn't quite understand what leaving him with paper means. Nobody understands that. I believe you do. I believe I do.

So that's the one way they could get Gordon Getty to abandon his dream of being in control of his father's company, and they did it, they did it. But they haven't gotten away with it yet.

So they got the museum to sell. And that's the last thing Gordon Getty told you. "I had no choice but to sell."

I thought that was sad. I really did.

You know, we build for our children. Fellow builds a company and wants his family to operate it and to run it. And along comes some people that he has made, has put in their positions and they turn on his family when he dies.

It happens. It happens.

Special Issue No. 2—before we got to that, I want to spend another minute with Mr. Tisch.

I just found out something in here about Mr. Tisch that he said in his testimony, and that is that what the—the question was—my question of Mr. Tisch—Mr. Lipton "And that's Mr. Lipton's description of the Pennzoil proposal as per the Copley notes on page 63?"

His answer: "Yes."

QUESTION: "All right. And that is what the board

voted on, was the proposal as stated on page 63 by Mr. Lipton?"

And his answer: "Yes."

Now, they want to tell you Mr. Tisch only said, well, price only.

But that's at page 20474 and 20476 of this transcript.

Indelibly inscribed. Can't be erased. Can't be edited.

And that's what he said.

Now, Mr. Tisch also testified that the converse of the condition in the memorandum of agreement by the museum would provide that if the board approved the memorandum of agreement, which he earlier said was what the board voted on, on page 63 of the Copley notes, then the museum was bound.

Ms. Vlahakis testified to the very same thing to you by her deposition.

That if the board approved that, they were then bound. I can't—they say they are bound. We say they are bound. Texaco says they are not, Texaco wasn't a party to that.

And you are obligated to determine that No. 1 issue based on what the Getty people thought at the time and the Pennzoil people thought at the time. And nothing else.

I had him read the part in the *Fortune* magazine aloud when he asked him and he looked at me.

I said, "What does 'a bird in the hand' mean to you?" And he looked at me kind of silly—like I was silly.

It was a silly question. Everybody knows that. And Mr. McKinley had testified he didn't.

And he said, "'Bird in the hand' means to me the same thing it means to everybody else, and the same thing it means to you."

And that's after cool reflection, a couple of weeks or so had passed and the chairman of the board of Getty knew what he voted on and what that board voted on.

And their champion, Mr. Petersen, that was running

that company so beautifully, until that point automatically became a dunce who didn't know what he was saying to these people. And never refuted it and never tried to.

And what about this congratulatory thing?

Mr. Lipton told you that Mr. Rohatyn, who is a partner of Mr. Glanville, the investment banker for Lazard-Freres and a very respected man, I asked him, do you deny—and I put it this way deliberately—having dealt with Mr. Lipton a day and a half or so?

"Do you deny calling Mr. Rohatyn in Sun Valley and saying congratulations, you have just made"—you, Lazard—"have just made the deal of the century, on January 4th?"

He says, "I don't recollect it, but I cannot deny that."

And he didn't.

And they made a big deal about Mr. Liman not being in that boardroom.

And the last deposition you heard, Mr. Siegal, saying, "Well, I remember he came in the boardroom after the meeting."

Mr. Tisch never denied it, because I shook hands with him.

"It was either—maybe it was just outside the boardroom. I can't remember."

And Mr. Tisch, along with Mr. Liedtke, got invited up to the Getty suite at the Pierre Hotel to drink champagne to celebrate the agreement.

Did Gordon Getty think at that time he had an agreement? Did Pennzoil? Did the museum?

It's not important what Texaco told you they thought. It's what they thought.

And the board had nothing to do with those two agreements between the museum and the trust except to either approve or not approve.

If not approved, it's gone. And they had two more weeks. There is no pressure to find another buyer.

No, they went out secretly shopping this thing, the thing the judge says they couldn't do. The thing that they swore in this deposition that they couldn't do under the Texaco proposal of agreement in principle.

Why was that different? You heard the testimony.

Petersen and someone else in answer to a question, No, we can't shop the deal.

And there's no board authorization anywhere that you will find in this evidence that says and gives authority to Boisi or anybody to go and shop this deal of Pennzoil's. None.

And isn't it strange that the only time in the history of that company that there are no board minutes that are ratified are the January 2nd and 3rd meetings to discuss Pennzoil and the January 6th meeting to discuss Texaco?

There are none.

This has never happened before.

The board wouldn't ratify them. Only conclusion, there are no minutes. Highly unusual.

Lipton told you he knew that Copley would know whether they reached an agreement, and Copley is the man that sent this message to Mr. Garber. Agreement.

Mr. Lipton testified that Mr. Williams signed that memorandum of agreement and he understood what that first sentence meant, plan approved and developed by the museum.

And he signed it. I don't know what else we can do with that.

I would like to take you now to Special Issue No. 2 and ask you to look at it for just a minute.

You can read it as well as I can. The evidence is replete.

Mr. McKinley admitted from the witness stand that the only reason the Pennzoil agreement was not finalized was the action of Texaco.

Do you need more than that? I just can't—interfere,

stop the train, don't sign up yet, hear from me, give indemnities, give special warranties.

The judge described all of that for you. It is interfering.

And then when I asked Mr. Lipton some questions about an article, an interview he had given that he admitted he read, that he said I never called him to correct it, didn't see anything that needed correction, never corrected it. And in it he said—he denied that he was haggling with McKinley in the lobby of New York's Pierre Hotel.

He denied that Gordon Getty decided with persuasion from Lipton to sign an agreement to sell his 40 percent of the Getty stock to Texaco.

He denied saying that he dealt exclusively with McKinley face-to-face in the Getty deal.

He denied saying that the big decision Mr. McKinley had to make was whether to improve his offer of $125 from $122.50 he had originally proposed.

He denied saying that Mr. McKinley told him, I will pay you $125 if you can get the skittish Gordon Getty to sign that night.

He denied saying that he, in fact, had been responsible for Gordon Getty having to abandon his dream of being the Getty who would once again run Getty Oil. He denied. He admitted the interview, but he denied it.

Now, Mr. McKinley also told you that he recognized that an agreement in principle is some sort of an agreement, some sort of understanding, some sort of intent.

He also says in this interference thing, he never asked anybody for the Copley notes.

He never asked Mr. Peterson as to how they voted.

He never asked anybody in the suite in the Pierre that night as to how the vote on Pennzoil came out at the Getty board meeting.

He did none of this, intentionally trying to avoid the ultimate answer he knew he would get. And he agreed to the indemnities and he agreed to the warranties, and he did more than that.

He knew what he was going to do on January 5th when he went to that Texaco board meeting and got that Texaco board of directors to indemnify him and Mr. Kinnear and Mr. Weitzel and Mr. DeCrane from any actions they might take in acquiring Getty.

That's what he did.

It's in their resolution.

And if it wasn't on their minds to do this underhanded thing, what was on their mind?

Now I want to talk to you about the damages. There has been no dispute about the damages in this case. None. You saw the models. And it's easy to figure.

If they had had anybody that would come—and they listed three damage experts, three of them, to come here and to tell you what their ideas about the damages were.

They didn't bring any of them.

They criticized us for not bringing some people, but I got those depositions somewhere and they want me to read that pile of depositions to you.

That's Mr. Barber and Mr. Cialone.

Now, do you want to hear that? I thought you were going to throw up listening to all the depositions you had to hear.

And they criticized us for that. They were here if they wanted them.

They could have had them. We produced those people for them.

But they didn't produce their experts.

So, unrefuted in this testimony is the damage model given you by the damage expert, Mr. Kerr, and Mr. Liedtke's assessment of the damages.

Finding and development costs, which is the reasonable one, $7.5 billion.

Texaco, through its lawyers, does not think you will

assess those kinds of damages. They think that you are not big enough to do that. I think you are.

I questioned you very carefully about this, as I recall, when we talked the first time we met.

You said nothing would deter you from that if the evidence preponderated in that way. Well, it not only preponderates, it's all the evidence. There is no other evidence.

So to suggest to you subtly that you are going to give something—they didn't say it, this is what he was meaning. This difference there in stock is what you are going to do. There is no evidence that this is the measure of damages and that would be insulting to you and to us.

It would not be following our oaths.

The only proof we have is that given to you by Mr.— I forget his name—

THE COURT: Barrow.

MR. JAMAIL: Mr. Tom Barrow. And that's our evidence. They could refute it if they had someone to refute it with.

To assess damages of any kind, it has to be a reason.

And you think about this case and the reason for the assessment of damages in this case are monumental. Not just that Pennzoil actually suffered this, but the way they suffered.

And I want to combine the punitive part along with the actual. The actuals are plain and simple.

You take a number that's historic for Pennzoil's finding and development costs. You subtract what they would have paid to acquire the three-sevenths of Getty and you multiply that by the number of barrels that they lost and that's their loss.

And they discounted it down to present cash value. It's $7.5 billion.

Now, I can't force any of you to do anything, and I am not that way anyway. Wouldn't try to. It's dumb.

But at this moment in time, you need to understand something. There cannot be half justice without there being half injustice. Pennzoil is entitled to full and complete compensation for its damages.

Full and complete. That's what Judge Casseb tells us. Not discounted because it's too much money with no evidence to support a discount.

I plead with you, if you are going to right this wrong, it has to be done here. It's not going to—this will never happen again because it's so expensive to bring one of these kinds of cases. So expensive. People just say well, okay, but you caught the wrong horse this time.

Hugh Liedtke is my friend. Baine Kerr is my friend, and I can't divorce myself from that. But I can't divorce myself from these facts, either. They honestly endeavored to build the company.

Hugh Liedtke, who got started with the help—with the help of J. Paul Getty.

You heard the testimony. The man who came to his wedding, stranger, interloper, going to rape the company?

He got his start from that family. Believed he could work with them. And could have, if his—it had not been sabotaged.

You people here, you jury, are the conscience, not only of this community now in this hour, but of this country.

What you decide is going to set the standard of morality in business in America for years and years to come.

Now, you can turn your back on Pennzoil and say, okay, that's fine. We like that kind of deal. That's slick stuff.

Go on out and do this kind of thing. Take the company, fire the employees, lose the pension fund. You can do a deal that's already been done, or you can say, no, hold it, hold it, hold it now.

That's not going to happen. I have got a chance. Me.

Juror. I have got me a chance. I can stop this. And I am going to stop it.

And you might pull this on somebody else, but you are not going to run it through me and tell me to wash it for you.

I am not going to clean that dirty mess up for you.

It's you. Nobody else but you. Not me. I am not big enough. Not Liedtke, not Kerr, not anybody. Not the judge. Only you in our system can do that. Don't let this opportunity pass you. Do not.

We have brought you evidence, honestly and fairly, conclusively showing that the intent of the parties that dealt that night, they intended to be bound.

The evidence is clear. Punitive damages is meant for one reason, to stop this kind of conduct.

If we were not entitled to ask you for punitive damages, we would not be able to stand before you now and request it.

It would have been stricken. Certain cases only can we ask for and receive punitive damages. This is one of them.

And the reason is that you can send a message to corporate America, business world, because it's just people who make up those things.

It isn't as though we are numbers and robots. We are people. And you can tell them that you are not going to get away with this.

The law says you should be punished if you did this and it's not only to punish you for this that you took, it is to deter others from doing the same thing.

Now, are we moralistic, smart enough to overcome all of the smoke screen, with all of the muscle Texaco has got spewed around here about the open points?

Where are they?

Judge Casseb does not ask you about that.

I ask you to remember that you are in a once-in-a-lifetime situation. It won't happen again.

It just won't happen.

You have a chance to right a wrong, a grievous wrong, a serious wrong.

It is going to take some courage.

You got that.

It's going to take a logical reexamination of what went on.

You don't have to read everything. You remember better than anybody what happened in this courtroom.

If you come to the conclusion, as I hope and believe that you will under all the evidence in this case, that a grievous wrong has been done to Pennzoil by reason of their undoing this binding agreement, this intent, this meeting of the minds these people had on these three elements the judge had asked you about, then no verdict less than $7.5 billion actual and $7.5 billion punitive is enough to dent them, because they saved from $40 to $60 billion by their own statement by taking Getty and for every billion dollars that you assess, it cost them 43 cents more per barrel than the purchase price of Getty.

I know you are going to do the right thing.

You are people of morality and conscience and strength.

Don't let this opportunity pass you.

How Others See Him

Kirk Douglas *Actor, Author*

Joe Jamail is himself a great actor. He plays the humble, ordinary guy who hides his genius. I always get a box of grapefruit from Joe at Christmas, beautiful grapefruit. I told him, Joe, those grapefruits are so good, you should buy the farm. He said he did.

I don't see Joe enough, but every so often we touch base. I have read all about his big trials, and I admired so much the way he conducted them. I wanted to play that part in a movie, but my speech is no longer clear enough since my stroke.

Every great lawyer has a bit of thespian in him. If Joe had been an actor, he would have been me.

JANET HANSEN *Colleague, Lawyer*

I usually mark the end of each year at Jamail and Kolius with a Christmas poem to the tune of "'Twas the Night Before Christmas." This started after the Pennzoil case when the *Wall Street Journal* ran an editorial entitled "Merry Christmas, Mr. Jamail." Each year we all contribute to a new poem with a summary of the events and cases of the past year, and Joe loves to hear it recited with gusto.

I start with Christmas because it is a good place to begin to describe the Joe we know at the office.

Joe is a man of simple likes. He likes his work. He likes his office and he likes the people who work for him. It took many years of Christmas gift searching to learn that Joe does not need, want, or care about most of the fancy, expensive things in life. Out of all our attempts to express our appreciation for him at the end of the year, he likes the simplest things best—a poem, a tomato, or a book. Any and all plaques or posters that say "King" are also good picks—even the homemade ones.

Joe brings his lunch to work every day. He makes it himself. If we are in trial, that brown bag is there too. He and Gus Kolius tell a story about leaving a tuna fish sandwich in a file cabinet in a particular courtroom they didn't like. On those rare days when Joe doesn't pack himself a lunch, he goes to the farmer's market. It is always enjoyable to go with him and watch the gleam in his eye as he wanders through the produce. He loves homegrown tomatoes. He has suppliers all over Texas, and he will drop everyone and everything to run out to League City to pick up a bushel. Some days we find a tomato on our desk and we know that Joe has just made a fresh haul.

There are many other easy, simple things that make Joe happy. A sunny and cool day, a good book, an apple or a peach, his fifty-year-old briefcase, and his favorite blue shirt. But we have learned not to be lulled into complacency. Just when you think you have him figured out, Joe does something to make you know how deeply you have erred and just how complex he really is.

Joe has handled a lot of big cases, and he has always done it with a small staff of lawyers and secretaries, all of whom have worked for him for a very long time—most more than twenty years. When Joe is getting ready for trial, everyone is involved. He insists on teamwork and he gets it. We walk around with our shoulders back or suffer the friendly Marine Corps poke. We do not wait for deadlines to file documents or responses or motions. We do it now and file it now. We start working on a voir dire months before a case is set for trial. Joe fine tunes it until the last moment. Every detail of a case that can be worked out and prepared before trial is done. He does not dictate details, but he is in charge of the overall production.

In trial, you have to be very careful when you are around Joe, whether you are on his side or not. I have had my "lucky trial purse" thrown like a football across the room when it is found in his space.

Another twenty-year lawyer in our office, who is now retired, David Bebout, once called Joe "weird" in response to a reporter's question. David was right. Joe truly is weird, and it is never more obvious than when he is in trial.

His ability to sense what a witness will say and get him or her to say it is scary. You can't imitate it and make it work—you just have to have it. Almost like an alien, he seems to be able to absorb energy from other people and know what they are thinking. This makes him highly effective with an adverse witness and highly annoyed with anyone within ten feet who is fidgeting or nervous or fumbling with papers. It was the experience of a lifetime to be in trial with Joe and Gus together. Their combined talents and knowledge transformed a trial into a symphony—Joe with his intellectual passion and Gus with his technical logic.

Sometimes the two approaches would become comedic, as when Gus, delivering an opening statement in a products case, had to tell the jury to forget everything they learned about the machine in voir dire from Joe because "Joe's mechanical abilities were limited to the folding of money."

Another former lawyer in our office, the late Nat B. King, who at the age of ninety retired from writing appeals, once fussed at Joe for introducing a volume of the United States Code of Criminal Procedure dealing with firearms into evidence at trial and asked him why in the world he had done that. Joe just said, "It was on the table." From then on Mr. King would tell anyone who would listen that Joe would offer anything into evidence that was not nailed down to the counsel table. He would warn me every time we were going to trial not to let Joe get his hands on any law books.

Of course, it was Mr. King who quoted *Alice in Wonderland* in a brief written for the United States Supreme Court—to the extreme delight and encouragement of his boss.

Joe has always had the vision and the talent to inspire the highest quality work out of everyone. He encourages, listens, praises, and thanks freely. He also questions, prods, pushes, never tires, and works harder than everyone around him. We all hate it when Joe answers the office telephone, because it usually means we have to look into a case that has no liability anywhere, except in his ever-optimistic mind.

Each morning Joe stops by every office and desk to say hello, drop off an apple, or check on whether you filed that brief yet. You do not have to be a lawyer to be asked to draft questions to witnesses or thoughts for an opening or closing statement. He is interested in everyone's ideas and input and expects everyone to contribute to the end result.

Behind the apparent simplicity with which he produces, directs, and prepares his trials is where the genius lies.

Joe is incredibly well read. He has a memory like a steel trap.

His interests vary from Mark Twain to the newspaper funnies. He knows history, understands it, learns from it, and applies it to his life and his work. He is always reading a book, and you can see the grin on his face and the gleam in his eye with the book in his hands. You will probably not hear him quote the prophets or scholars over scotch—but the knowledge is there.

It is what he draws on and uses to help him read and understand people. He actually has a genuine interest in people, how they feel, what they think, and how they react. This is both a talent and a curse because people can make him nuts—when confronted with the arrogant, the stupid, or the narrow-minded, Joe has two choices: either stay and cuss or walk away and drink.

Joe is also completely fearless. I don't know where he got this trait. I know you can't acquire it or learn it. The larger the adversary or the obstacle, the harder Joe will fight to overcome it. He hates bullies—people bullies, corporate bullies, insurance bullies, law-firm bullies, government bullies, all bullies. Bullies make Joe fight harder.

Joe will say anything. Anywhere. In front of anyone. He also has an answer for anything and everyone. In one of our lunchtime discussions about religion, many years ago, Joe actually told me what I should do if I got to the gates of heaven on Judgment Day and found myself being turned away. I should tell God that "if I was supposed to be doing something down there that I wasn't, you should have given me a bigger sign!" I have never forgotten that advice.

Around Jamail & Kolius, each Christmas, we will be

working on another poem and trying to find that "perfect present." There really isn't anything he needs—or wants. How do you thank someone each year for giving you a great career with a front-row seat to the greatest legal brilliance on earth? He has been much more than an employer. He has been a teacher, a defender, an advisor, a coach, a father, an uncle, a psychologist, and a friend.

It just isn't possible to relate every story, every case, every settlement. He has closed bad hospitals and unscrupulous businesses. He has stopped the production of dangerous drugs and defective products. He sued the same crane manufacturer twice, ten years apart, for injuries to two different crane operators caused by the same crane. Since the Pennzoil verdict against Texaco, Joe has represented and advised many Texaco employees.

He has represented widows, widowers, children, poor people, rich people, lawyers, judges, small businesses, and large law firms. He has made big fees, and he has taken no fee when there is not enough money available to take care of an injured person or their family. He has given his time and money to schools, universities, children's programs, hospitals, and the courts. Quite simply, Joe likes being a lawyer. He is proud to be a lawyer. And he is unquestionably the best.

G. P. (GEEP) HARDY *Lawyer, Rancher, Loyal Friend*

Joe Jamail is truly a man for all seasons. He cannot sing, play a musical instrument, or paint, and he is not what one would call man of letters. He is, however, the most adroit observer of human behavior I have ever known. That he does not possess the attributes of the Renaissance man does not make Joe less a man for all seasons. His understanding of human nature gives him incredible insight into the arts, into business practices, entertainment law (an area of special expertise), politics, religion, and, most importantly, family.

Clearly, Joe Jamail is one the legal icons of his generation, if not the century. If one were to say he has an "ear" for the law, it would be an understatement. He has an incredible guessing average. While his exploits both in and out of the court are legendary, those exploits pale in comparison to the results he has achieved in representing his clients. If one were to characterize Joe's love of the law, one would have to start with his love and loyalty to his clients.

Joe has priorities. First, his family, then his clients, and third his friends. A person could not ask for a more devoted friend, always willing to share his most valuable asset with his friends, his advice. (I personally would prefer money, but his advice has translated nicely into money.) No man could be more devoted to his family than Joe.

He worships his sons, Dahr, Randall, and Rob, but the light of his life is his wife of more than forty-five years, Lilly Mae (Lee). The love Joe has for Lee is as obvious as her love for Joe. They hold hands and look at each other like two people who have shared not only the heartaches and happiness of a lifetime, but whose souls are bound together for all eternity. When they look at each other it is with absolute devotion and caring love.

Joe's devotion to Lee has cost his friends dearly. Many a night Joe went home to Lee and left the rest of us in the bar. The friend that he is, he would call the very next morning to make sure we made it home all right.

It's not as bad as it might seem. Joe always closed out the tab before he left, so we had to make the conscious decision to reopen the tab.

In the not-distant past, a group of us would get together in the afternoons and celebrate Joe's latest victory. Unfortunately for us, it was an almost-every-afternoon occasion. We celebrated Pennzoil for well over a year. It almost put several of us out of business celebrating Joe's victories. Nevertheless, he would occasionally share a pearl of wisdom that would keep our boat afloat. What a privilege to sit and learn from Joe Jamail, W. James Kronzer, Harry Reasoner, Ron Krist, and others. A fellow could learn more in one afternoon than in a semester of law school or a lifetime of practice.

Joe has my respect, not only because he is my friend, but because he is truly a moral man who values his ethics above any asset he possesses. There just aren't many folks you can say that about.

DAHR JAMAIL *Lawyer, First Son*

In his seventies, Joe still has many characteristics that he always possessed: a strong will, pride, ego, energy, and restlessness. But one thing stands out. In many ways he has the components of a young boy.

He can be like a kid in the way he views himself. He loves his free time, and he could have as much as he wants, but he limits it and then makes the most of what he takes. He loves his car, Galveston, whiskey, hanging out with people who can laugh. Except for his plane, he isn't much for fancy stuff. But most of all he loves his family and his work.

The Jamails had been in the grocery business for forty years before Joe was born. On Saturdays, even now, he goes to the market and argues about the price of produce. He likes to pick out his own fruit and vegetables, and he knows how to get the best.

For many years, in the afternoon after work, he would meet with great lawyers and judges to discuss and debate legal issues or problems with the people involved in on-going cases. Unfortunately, there are only a few of that caliber of judges and lawyers still alive. Now his friends and fellow lawyers are much younger than Joe. He likes to be with them, but I know he misses friends like Judge George Cire, Jim Kronzer, Curtis Brown, Spurgeon Bell, Charles Crady. So many are gone. Thinking about the past is like walking through a graveyard.

Others, like Gus Kolius, Tom Stovall, and Dick Miller, have hung it up, playing golf and fishing and doing whatever retired lawyers and judges do.

Joe can't give up the courtroom. It is the venue for his craft and his skills: his hunger for winning and his feeling of power are at the highest and most intense level in this simple place. When he is there, it is life-and-death. Nothing else matters.

The quiet, driving force behind him is his love for his wife and family. Although abrasive and rough, he has always been able to maintain his wonderful balance, instilling his own fundamental principles of right and wrong without his sons sacrificing their individuality.

His love, admiration, and respect for Lee is foremost, even over his children. She is always first, always will be, and should be.

They have always had a very outgoing social life and have been active in public service. They are strong supporters of the University of Texas and the school's winningest coach, Darrell Royal.

For many nights, from the time I was fourteen, Dad and the coach would be up all night with Willie Nelson playing guitar. Each has been the very best at what he did. They are an unlikely but inseparable trio, Joe, Darrell, and Willie, Texas legends all.

Willie is the master musician. Royal's teams rarely lost games they were favored to win, and Joe Jamail lost even fewer cases. They knew they could perform. They had the skills to back up their confidence, and their believers were far and wide.

I would wake up for school and they would still be at it: Willie still picking his guitar, the coach drinking a beer and a bowl of chili cold out of the fridge. Joe would be showered, shaved, and preparing to go to his office. He would be fresh and alert, as if nothing out of the ordinary had taken place.

RANDALL JAMAIL *Music Producer, Second Son*

I have been blessed all my life. Although my life is independent from my parents', I cannot separate those blessings from them. I have so many memories of my dad, both fond and funny (or at least they seem funny now), and always vivid.

There are far too many to list, and they are much too personal for their full weight to be appreciated by someone reading mere words. Also, reminiscing conjures a life from the past, and I can't keep up with the one he is living. Anyway, he always taught me to remember the past but not to dwell on it. Instead, he encouraged me to look ahead to what I will do next. I will say this: He is wonderfully unpredictable. Even today, when the phone rings, I do not know whether he is calling to talk about baseball or to rip my head off because he doesn't like the sloppy condition of the front door of my house.

He has always been an amazing teacher of the simplest yet hardest-learned lessons of life: courage, honesty, justice, and compassion. He taught me that it is better to be punished for the truth then to escape with a lie. The liar never stands alone but is always chased by the ghosts of his lie.

He insisted that I fight for those principles that were just and have the compassion to recognize when another was being treated unfairly, and he demanded that I have the courage to fight those who would maintain the status quo which caused such injustice. He demanded that we respect our mother, as the strongest and most loving member of our family. I recall countless times my father saying to me, "If it weren't for your mother, I would . . ."

It was always exciting growing up in our house. We never knew who my parents might bring home, but there were always lots of people: lawyers and judges, of course, but also artists, athletes, politicians, musicians, and authors. It was a wonderful way to grow up. I was never lacking for inspiration. In our house, one learned quickly to be a conversationalist, and the kitchen was the main forum.

While my parents did not take us every time they went somewhere, they did take us everywhere. We were exposed to the world as a place of beauty and magic. Because we are citizens of that world, they never let us forget that the effort to make it a better place is the best use of any human being's talent. Through his constant example, we learned that to try, without reaching the original goal, is still success. To not try, for fear of failing, is failure.

No one will dispute that when it comes to living life to its fullest, on the scale from one to ten, Joe scores an eleven.

ROB JAMAIL *Business Manager, Third Son*

To describe our dad is as difficult as describing natural instincts. You feel it, know it, love, use, and cherish it, but you certainly can't put it into words. The easiest way I can start my description is to begin with how he got here.

My dad was born in Houston in 1925, the second of five children. His parents were immigrants. My grandfather, Joe, came to Houston around the turn of the century. He was a boy raised by two older brothers. Later, he served in the U.S. Army in France during the First World War. When he came home, he met and very quickly married my grandmother, Marie. She had only recently arrived in the United States. My dad grew up in the east side of Houston and attended only Catholic schools. After high school graduation in 1942, he joined the Marines. After the war, he went back to the University of Texas to finish undergraduate and law school.

While a student, he met, tried to date, and fell in love with my mother. They were married in 1949.

We were raised about like any other kids who were born in the 1950s and were teen- and college-aged in the 1970s. We had more than most kids, but my parents tried to make sure our priorities were right. Our suburban neighborhood was considered way out in the boondocks at that time, with some great neighbors. My dad's best friend, George Cire (the judge), lived about a block away, and we always did things with his family.

As a parent, my dad could be described as hands-off. He would let us do almost anything as long as we did not hurt ourselves. Of course, he kept his eye on us in case there was any real danger. Every kid on our street from about the age of ten and up knew to call him when they were in a legal jam, and we got the calls. He could handle any situation, and everybody knew it.

He could be sympathetic and helpful if there was trouble, but not so if you were stupid. My dad does not suffer stupid people gladly. He and Mom love us, and there is no limit to how far they would go for any of us, and sometimes it could be a l-o-o-o-o-n-g way.

One of my most vivid childhood memories is of my father and George Cire sitting around the kitchen table, with at *least* one bottle of whiskey, discussing law the way other guys talk about a college football road game at Notre Dame ("That 9th District is harder than anything over there"—"Yes, they're a bunch of assholes"). They loved it. My dad was meant to practice law and probably nothing else. He was not a little league-coach or a school parent.

He would not survive today's daily hands-on routine of car pools, ballet, and soccer. His genetic code was not set up to do such things. He spends time with young lawyers now, but I think he misses the interaction with his contemporaries and dislikes how the practice of law has become institutionalized.

My dad always made fun of himself when he talked about growing up. He told us all the stupid stuff he did, flunking a law school class or going AWOL while in the Marines. The stories were hilarious. As an adult now, I think it was his way of not putting any pressure on us to do one thing or another. He was trying to show us that we were just as smart, but not all of those genes got passed down.

I knew by about the seventh or eighth grade that I did not want to practice law. I am sure my parents knew it also. My dad would be the first to say that practicing law is not for everybody. He can show you several of his contemporaries who practiced twenty years and then went on to do something different (like go nuts). He likes to create the appearance that what he does is easy—he's a loose cannon with his mouth. And some people might believe that his career has been effortless because all they ever saw were news clips from high-profile cases.

The reality is that he works hard, is very smart, and is extremely disciplined. He might have three or four drinks at night, but it's at the same time every night, and that is extremely disciplined. He's not wild or crazy. He has tried more cases than anyone, but settled more.

A smart guy knows when to fight and when to deal. You don't practice law for fifty years and have the clients he has represented without knowing what you are doing.

He has always had good people around him, friends, co-workers, and most importantly, our mother. For the last fifty years, she has been able to keep a handle on things. He was gone a lot, trying a case almost every week, and she had to take care of us by herself. There is no way he could have accomplished all he that he did without her. She's as smart as he is. That goes back to intelligence; you have to know how to choose—and she was his smartest choice.

GUS KOLIUS *Lawyer, Philosopher*

When Joe started in private practice, I was doing defense work with Fulbright Crooker and we tried three suits against each other. We split two and settled the other.

We were friends, and we tried to work our cases out. I think I'm the only lawyer he admits to losing a case to, but that's just Joe. Winning was serious business. He is tremendously competitive and he likes people who are. His cases are competitive from the first filing of the first instrument. Nothing went smoothly if you were on the other side of the table.

In 1969, I left Fulbright and decided I was never going to work full-time again. So I walked into Jamail's office wearing a Hawaiian shirt and asked Joe if he wanted a part-time lawyer. It would turn out to be a wonderful experience for me. When I graduated from college I didn't have any connections. I was a sort of an itinerant lawyer for four or five years.

Fulbright gave me the opportunity to try lawsuits for seventeen years, and I didn't mess with the politics part of it.

There are no office politics around Joe Jamail. Starting out, he had won some hard lawsuits, had begun to make a name for himself. I had no academic interest in the law. It was a way to make a living, a pretty good living.

The first thing I did for Joe was to provide a good feel for mechanical problems, looking at the records. He doesn't have enough patience to look through records, or the dexterity to deal with machinery. I have said that Joe's dexterity was limited to folding money. We had a lot of product liability cases, refinery accidents and explosions and fires. I worked in factories and on airplanes and have a knack for those cases.

We made a good team and had a good time. Besides my brother, Joe is the best male friend I've ever had. I told him I would work six months a year. My wife and I were living on a boat in 1969, and I told him I would come back during hurricane season. The boat was named *Jason,* and I guess I was looking for the Golden Fleece.

Joe made two trips with me. One time, he met me in Panama City, when I was bringing the boat back from Florida. The first thing he did was to bring a bunch of groceries with him. He likes to cook. We dived for bay scallops. We must have eaten a bushel of them. Then we got as far as Orange Beach, Alabama, a day and a half out, and he was standing on the deck with a pair of binoculars and saw a pay phone. He couldn't pass it up. Said he had to make a call. Goes to the phone, calls Judge John Singleton, who had witnessed an accident in Austin that crippled a guy and wanted Joe to represent him.

So Joe called a cab in Mobile, sixty-seven miles away, to come pick him up. That was his first boat trip with me. The second one, he flew in with Lee to a little island called Samuel Cay in the Bahamas. We had two really nice days, maybe three. I kept telling him to wear shoes, and he went barefooted, cut his foot, got it infected, and had to leave.

So he doesn't have much tenure on a boat.

Joe works in short bursts. He needs to be around people. We never discussed what kind of financial arrangement we would have. We agreed that I would work when I wanted, or when he needed me. I never asked Joe for a penny. He was always more than fair with me. We never had an oral contract, never had a piece of paper, not a thing that would be an official agreement.

He added my name to the firm's title, but I never put in a penny into his office and we never had a true partnership. I don't recall asking why he did this, but I think it had to with our respect for each other. I was one of the few people he was ever associated with that Joe would listen to . . . in some ways. He would ask me for advice and I would tell him what I thought. We had a hell of a mutual respect. But he paid the rent and paid the staff and we didn't split anything on any formal basis. Joe would give me a check and I wouldn't know for sure if the money were a percentage of anything, or from which case.

I wasn't a partner, but I wasn't an employee, and I had no responsibility except to help Joe. It was wonderful for me. He is the most generous guy I have ever known.

Early in our friendship, Joe had a lawsuit for the captain of a tugboat that capsized. The captain cut himself up some and Joe represented him against the owners of the tugboat under the Jones Act.

I had handled maritime cases for Fulbright Crooker, and the defendant was a company I had represented. But this time they had hired another lawyer because they felt my fees were too high.

Before Joe went to trial, he called and told me about it. That was the first I had heard about it. He said, "Listen, I never have tried one of these admiralty cases. Will you help me prepare the charge?"

I said, "Come on over to the office." So he came over and I helped him prepare the charge. This was a case worth maybe twenty or thirty thousand dollars, and the verdict was for one hundred thousand-plus. So the day after the verdict came in, the lawyer for the insurance company called me and said, "Look, this is a terrible verdict. Will you defend it on appeal?"

I said, "Yeah, I'd be interested in handling it, but first let me find out something about the case." I waited a day or two and called him back and said, "I tell you what I will do. I think I can settle this case for you if you send me a check for $75,000." I walked over to Joe's office and said, "I represent this outfit now, and it's obvious you got a fraudulent verdict."

He said, "What do you mean?"

I said, "Well, the charge is improper."

Joe said, "You SOB, you helped prepare it. I'm not going to settle."

I said, "Well, you got to tell your client about it because I'm going to leave the check here." I charged the insurance company a fee, got my client back, and Joe settled for $50,000 more than the case was worth. Everyone was happy except the other lawyer.

Another time, we were trying a case in a little town called Cold Springs, in San Jacinto County, between Lufkin and Houston on Highway 59. The population was so sparse they only had about fifty qualified jurors. Steve Buckman was the third lawyer, from Beaumont. The morning we settled the case the three of us went over to Sue's café, the only place there that sold beer. It was ten in the morning, and we drank beer until about four. Had to drive back, and figured we better get something to eat. A waitress with a dirty uniform, standing there scratching her crotch and picking her nose, held out her scratch pad and said, "What are you boys going to have?" I said, "Bring me a coconut, or a banana or a hard-boiled egg, and I'll peel it myself."

They threw our asses out. Joe had a brand-new Buick Riviera with a police interceptor in it. He also had an ice box full of beer. So when they ran us out of the restaurant, we went to the car and I asked Joe for a beer or two to help me survive the drive, and he wouldn't let me have one. He took off, burning rubber, and I drove off at a more leisurely place.

About five or six miles down the road, there was Joe pulled over by the side of the road. He had run into a buzzard. Said he was going 125 miles an hour when he hit the buzzard and shattered his windshield. He was lucky it didn't kill him. There was blood, guts, feathers, everything all over the inside of that new car. And so he said, "I need a lift." He wasn't hurt at all. He was just filthy.

I said, "Take off your clothes, I'm not going to let you get in my car with all that bloody mess on you." He got in the car in his shorts and put the beer in the front seat.

I took him home, and he said, "You don't need to get out."

I said, "Oh, no, I don't want to miss this when Lee sees you." He went up the steps with his clothes under his arm, standing there in his shorts, and Lee came to the door. She looked at him and said—I'll never forget it— "Oh, honey, so this is what the practice of law looks like. Did you have a bad day?"

RONNIE KRIST *Lawyer, Friend*

Fate is a strange thing. It led me to Joe Jamail thirty years ago, when another lawyer sued me for a large fee I had earned, claiming that the case was in fact his. This was an unjust accusation, but I needed a friend and help. This was my first significant fee, and not only had I earned and deserved it, but my young family and I really needed it.

My law office was located directly next door to the

local 7-Eleven back then, so I could hardly afford the consequences of a protracted battle. For a brief moment, I feared that I might end up working *inside* the 7-Eleven instead of next door if I didn't come up with a solution to this career-altering assault.

At the time of this brutal attack on my livelihood, I was a total unknown and barely knew Joe, but at the urging of a friend, I called him for advice. I was hardly the first person—and certainly not the last—to call Joe Jamail with a seemingly unwinnable situation where a bully was involved. With a gravelly Texas accent, he told me that he would be glad to take the case, but he wouldn't accept a "damn dime" from me. It was clear he did not like the other guy and, further, felt he was overreaching and wrong. Admittedly, his charity might have been colored by the fact that Joe would probably throw all of his acquaintances in the water for the pleasure of fishing them out. Joe simply likes to be needed and loves to help. Still, he fished me out that day without a second thought, and of course, Joe *won*. Even more telling is the fact that he has never to this day implied any form of indebtedness. Joe gains great satisfaction from helping others, especially if it is a friend or underdog.

Our friendship was buoyed by somewhat common backgrounds. We both had parents one generation removed from the old country. Both families were merchants. Mine were tailors and his were grocers. This hearty immigrant-merchant connection is partly responsible for Joe's many gifts as a trial lawyer (as well as for his oft-expressed love of good produce). Joe's ability to artfully haggle and persuade were perhaps inherited traits that his grandfather never would have guessed would lead to such abundant success in American courtrooms, which, incidentally, was a place of great reverence to embattled immigrants.

This background also resulted in Joe's profound gratefulness for the opportunity to work hard at something he loves and still be paid handsomely. One cannot work as hard and as long as Joe has unless one indeed loves, boundlessly, his work. Joe happens to be a perfect fit. He is in precisely the right position to accentuate his talents. He would not have fared nearly as well in any other undertaking. He certainly would not have flourished in the buttoned-down world of corporate law; despite his considerable talent, he likely would have been thrown out for misbehavior or for failing to report his billable hours properly.

Over the years, our friendship has grown as we have recycled worn-out war stories and traded incessant phone calls over cases. We have jointly taken on cases, shared the workload, and enjoyed the experience. Joe always willingly did more than his part. We attended and participated in many seminars for the distinguished bar, as well as unofficial seminars at undistinguished bars, which incidentally were usually more educational and far more entertaining. Perhaps we celebrated Joe's multibillion-dollar verdict of the mid-eighties a bit too much, shortening my drinking life by several years as a matter of survival.

Also high on our unofficial priority list were the Saturday-morning football phone calls when the betting lines were analyzed. During the life of the venerable, and greatly missed, Jim Kronzer, it was a three-way conversation as we toiled in fallow fields, pooling our feeble talents in an effort to "pick a winner" and beat the bookie. Although we rarely did, hope springs eternal and continues to this day.

Although I am certain that *lucky* is a term seldom used to quantify Joe's football picks, it is sometimes jealously used to describe his many trial achievements. The word, although understandable in the face of Joe's overwhelming success, unfairly ignores the drive to succeed and natural talent that he had, even if it wasn't always apparent when he was younger. Joe's law school torts professor gave him a D, proving, to every law professor's chagrin, that skill as a trial lawyer can't be easily measured or predicted, especially in an academic environment.

Instead, it seems the best trial lawyers share the common desire to prove others wrong and stand up for those who have been wronged, even if it means taking on a pack of pit bulls with one hunting dog. Joe certainly possesses these qualities, as well as a fervent desire to see justice done.

The degree of talent, resiliency, and tenacity one possesses in the courtroom can serve as either testament or tombstone to winning. Joe's career has been defined by these traits. Few lawyers commandeer the courtroom with Joe's energetic drive, directed and focused on a solitary goal, and fewer still possess his relentless competitive zeal. In this day and age, it is hard to find a lawyer who cares more about the very act of trying and winning a lawsuit in the single-minded way that Joe does. Perhaps that is why those who have met him in the courtroom might wince at the memory while still looking back on the whole occasion with a certain stinging admiration.

Many advance the notion that one is only as good as his last victory. After the *Pennzoil* case, one might think it would have been a good time, and not an inappropriate age, for Joe to call it quits and retire to the sidelines. The accolades and the money he earned would certainly have lured most lawyers to happily retreat into the shadows earned from hard-fought success. But, in typical Joe fashion, he continues to this day to try cases. He approaches these cases with the vigor that one rarely sees from an excited lawyer in the infancy of his career, much less from a veteran of Joe's standing. His passion for challenges, it seems, will not be slowed by the passage of time.

Joe, like most of us, is not everything wonderful to

everybody. He has more than a few critics. But, as an unknown author once fittingly pointed out:

> If you have no enemies, alas, my friend,
>   the boast is poor because those that mingle
>   in the fray that the brave endure must have
>   made foes.
> If you have none, small is the work that you
>   have done.
> You've smote no traitor on the hip.
> You've dashed no cup from perjured lips.
> You've never changed a wrong to right.
> You've been a coward in the fight.

Yes, in his pursuit, Joe might have made enemies, but even the most cynical among them have never claimed that he was a coward in the fight. Admittedly, sometimes Joe honors moderation more by its breach than its enforcement. But, in one way at least, Joe is utterly uncomplicated. Although some feel irreverence is his hallmark, with Joe, what you see is what you get. You will never turn your back and wonder what he meant or whether he likes you, because he will already have told you point blank.

Say what you will, Joe's approach does get his point across—with, I might add, an economy of words. Some may take offense, but as Schopenhauer said, "Everybody's friend is nobody's." Joe would rather be a loyal friend to one than a hypocrite to many.

Joe has worked hard and fought with honor. He has represented the tattered of our society as well as corporate giants, giving to both equal care and concern, and above all always being solely beholden to his client and his client alone. He possesses a hatred of injustice and comfortably relates to the underdog with a heart of equality rather than superiority.

Profane but sincerely concerned, blunt but equally eloquent, unpredictable but always ethical, harsh but philan-thropic, Joe is a maze of contrarian twists. But when one shakes out the good, the bad, and the ugly, in the pantheon of trial lawyers, Joe Jamail stands alone.

HUGH LIEDTKE *Retired CEO, Pennzoil*

I don't believe that Joe Jamail and I ever spent a minute discussing business, his or mine, until the Texaco case. Of course, Joe had quite a reputation as a trial lawyer long before that lawsuit came along.

Our friendship was strictly social until I asked him to head up Pennzoil's legal team. We would run across each other down at Galveston now and then, do a little fish-ing and a little drinking. Except for that, his interests were quite different from mine, and his politics are quite different, that's a fact. I'm a conservative. He is a bleed-ing-heart liberal. You never had to guess where Joe stood, and I guess that is one reason we always got along well.

People in the oil industry were surprised when I hired Joe. He had no experience in oil and gas law and had never tried a takeover suit, but that was exactly why I wanted him. The case was kind of unusual in that it involved a huge corporation on the other side, and huge corporations have lots of friends in lots of places. I thought it was in Pennzoil's interest to have representation by someone who could not be accused of having any interest other than Pennzoil.

Jamail had not represented us before, and had not represented any other oil company, as far as I knew. Baker Botts had done most of our legal work, a superb law firm with excellent corporate lawyers and trial lawyers. But in this case I thought we needed someone beyond criticism in terms of any prior relationships.

Trial lawyers are different. The really good ones, I used to kid Joe, you feed them raw meat and gunpowder.

They have to be tough, usually quick thinkers, and willing to go for the jugular vein.

There was no question that Joe had no axe to grind when our deal to acquire Getty Oil was undone by a secret higher offer from Texaco. Secondly, he had one of the finest hands-on trial reputations of any lawyer around. When I asked him to take the case, he didn't show any enormous enthusiasm for it, didn't go charging into the fray. He had talked to a few people and he knew it wouldn't be easy. I think Joe responded in part to my anger, my conviction that we were right. And part of it was the challenge. To him that's always a factor.

But he agreed to take the case, and I never really cared what persuaded him. I just wanted him to take it.

From the first sign of what Texaco had done, we had other lawyers in New York. In fact, we had lawyers running out of our ears. One of the New York lawyers had said, "Look, in your position they will give you $200 million easy, and you can walk away, let it got at that." I was furious, frankly. I didn't agree with any of the advice I was getting. I thought Texaco was dead wrong and the law would get them. My background was in law. My father was a lawyer. I happen to believe in the system, and I was not going to turn them loose.

That would have been the easiest case in the world if not for the amount of damages. It was a simple contract case. And I mean simple. You just multiply what you didn't get by what oil was trading for a barrel, and that was it. The amount of damages, billions of dollars, that was difficult. The average guy in his lifetime is not very apt to be involved in that kind of money. It's awfully hard for people to realize the size of the deal we had negotiated with Getty—that was enormous. For the average man in the street, the amounts would numb your mind.

The jury could have reacted with fear (of the numbers). Deep down, as far as I'm concerned, it was a marvelous win legally, but we lost, basically, because we lost the company (Getty Oil). It was worth more than $3 billion.

The newspapers chose to take the view that we had an oral contract, period. We had a good deal more. We had a written contract. It did not have all the little niceties filled in, but the principal things, the price, the number of barrels, were all in there. And it was all signed and approved by the Getty board, with one exception. Approved by the Getty Museum and approved by our board. It was more than an oral contract.

The first thing I heard about Texaco getting into the picture, I was asleep in my hotel room in New York, and our general counsel knocked on my door, woke me, came into the room, and handed me the *New York Times*. He said, "Here it is." I woke up real fast. That morning I called and talked to a lot of people—lawyers in New York, our own corporate lawyers, and sometime that morning I talked to Joe.

I was angry, of course, but my reaction was to get all the facts and find out what in the hell had happened and what in the world were they relying on. And, in fact, what Texaco had done, because they had done a lot behind our backs. The lawyer for the Getty Museum, which owned a block of the stock, was supposed be drawing up our contract when, in fact, he was drawing up one for Texaco.

The first day was mainly spent assessing where we were, what the damages were, and then listening to the New York lawyers recommend that we settle for something around $200 million. And I'm sure that Texaco was confident this little piss-ant company would jump at it.

That was pennies per barrel. Texaco made it quite clear that they had the deal and they were going to take a very tough stand with us. You never know, they might have won the case if they hadn't been so arrogant. I will say one thing that lawsuit has done is to cause Texaco to want to improve their public image.

I'm a strong believer in deciding what you want to do and who you are going to use and then leave them the hell alone. I made no effort to influence what Joe was doing. Once, when I was testifying, I got mad at the other side's attorneys, and Joe jumped on me about it. He asked the judge for a recess and then told me to stop it, I was hurting his case. I was getting snappish with my answers, resenting the attorney's innuendoes, like he knew a secret that the jury didn't know and he can't come right out and tell them. I was pretty sore. But I listened to Joe.

He said if I didn't, to keep an eye on his rear end, because it would be going out the door.

Joe is supremely gifted, exudes total confidence, and I have never seen him indicate less than that. One of his big things as a trial lawyer, when he's in the courtroom there is no question about who is running it. The first thing Judge Sol Casseb did was look at him and announce, "Now, Joe, I want you to understand that I run this court." Said it to the other side, too. But he and Joe were good friends.

Another reason he is so good, he has an empathy with people that few lawyers have. He can pretty well tell what you're thinking just by talking to you. When he chooses a jury, no one does it better.

Every year a bunch of independent oilmen, called the All-American Wildcatters, have a "Strength Through Joy" meeting at a spa somewhere. They gave me an award that year. The club's motto is "My Word Is My Bond." Joe pretty much hammered that phrase into the jurors' minds.

When the jury came in, I was sitting behind Joe and the other lawyers, Jim Kronzer and John Jeffers and Irv Terrell, and Arthur Lyman, from New York. My wife was with me, and Lee was there

I personally felt we would win. The thing that surprised me was that they went a hundred percent on the damages. I thought they would whack them somewhere because Texaco made it clear they didn't think the jurors could understand it. They understood it a lot better than I thought they would.

By the time Texaco had exhausted all their legal remedies, except the very thin hope of having the Supreme Court throw it out, I knew where our line in the sand was: three billion, one hundred million.

We had gone through all the tough stuff—the Texas Supreme Court, all the appellate courts in the federal system. We could settle for this figure or we could continue to fight. Both companies had to face the same question. Did Texaco want to fight to the bloody, bitter end and risk losing everything they had?

They could keep you in court forever. Or is it smarter to go ahead and settle it and get on with your business? So we finally got it settled.

Pennzoil is a company that is over a hundred years old. Getty is also over a hundred years old. J. Paul Getty didn't start the company; his father, George, did. It was an amalgamation of companies, Skelly Oil, Sun Ray, Mission Oil. What people will fail to understand is the element of time. Time is invaluable in trying to put something together, and you pay nothing for it, basically. You pay so much for an asset, but you don't pay for the time it takes to get the asset.

This is a long way of saying that if we had had the entire $11 billion (the jury awarded), we could not have put together a Getty Oil Company with that, not in a reasonable period of time. You just can't do it. Give me fifty or sixty years and we could. Three billion dollars to Texaco was nothing. That's what was so hard for people to understand.

That's why I say that in the end we lost. Certainly, we had a lot of heart balm, I guess, but we didn't accomplish what we wanted. If you were trying to build a company, you missed.

In the international oil business, you have to have

staying power. The Chinese, for example, are very polite, but you may wind up sitting on something for years. Went over there several times, once with Joe and Lee. Our destination was actually Istanbul, and I got this message saying a deal we had going at the time was in trouble and I had to rush to Peking, and would I go? So I got hold of Joe and talked him into going. We arrived in Hong Kong and they had all our papers ready for us, and the oil minister, a fellow named Tonka, who was a Mongol, had a small dinner party and he and Joe were living it up.

Joe had served in the South Pacific with the U.S. Marine Corps, and they got to talking and drinking. Each time, there would be a toast in Chinese meaning "down the hatch." The next thing I know, Joe was talking to the oil minister, "As one old Jap killer to another," and the translator was laughing his head off.

JOHN MARTEL *Lawyer, Author*

About Joe Jamail: One thinks first about his generosity of spirit. Behind the occasional bluster (yes, he has been known to go over the top a time or two) and his celebrated powerful presence lurks a heart of gold, an inner gentleness, and, yes, even humility. Only the IRS knows how many millions of dollars he and Lee have donated to worthy causes, but those of us who have been the beneficiaries of his friendship are even more fortunate. (It must be said that those who are not his friends—people who have aroused his animus—are sometimes not so fortunate.)

Joe is a loving man who is not afraid to express his affection. When you have been hugged by Joe Jamail, you know you have been hugged.

Loyalty. Joe is loyal and stands behind his word. Accordingly, he commands the loyalty of his staff and friends.

Humor. Next, I think of his humor, his love of laughter, his willingness to laugh at himself. I chuckle every time I think of his client's car smashing its way through cement chickens like a bowling ball striking pins or about trying to get his favorite vegetable served in his own home. You will not be in Joe's presence long until the joy of laughter fills the room.

Trial work. Joe understands that jury work is performance, that the law—rules and regulations—can be learned, but understanding what people want to hear, and when and how they want to hear it, is a gift that few enjoy. Indeed, few who have practiced trial advocacy in our country's history have possessed this gift in greater measure. Joe is the consummate jury trial lawyer.

BERNARD RAPAPORT *Philanthropist*

More than almost any person I know, Joe understands that capitalism is the best economic system ever conceived by the mind of man because it recognizes the greed instinct in all of us.

No, I wouldn't want Joe to be the English teacher for my two grandchildren, nor would I want him to be in charge of their etiquette training. That is not his field, because he chooses for it not to be. When it comes to his brainpower, his success as a lawyer affirms incontrovertibly that he was blessed with more than his share.

That's not why I love him. He also knows that democracy is the best political system ever conceived because it recognizes the necessity of being cooperative. So with his brilliance, he comprehends that it is only the integration of the two systems that makes possible a sustaining society.

He hates greed—a greed that produces the injustices that seek to destroy our society. He has the most intense sense of outrage of injustice of any person I know. You might say he almost fitfully employs every resource within him to combat it, to destroy it, to fight it, and no one does it better than he.

He is not one of these do-gooders. He knows the significance of Samuel Johnson's observation "They may talk like angels, but they act like men." He never loses touch with reality. Although he has made a lot of money, he doesn't count it or covet it. Yet those who are perpetrating injustices had better be aware that Joe Jamail will make them pay in a way they never dreamed possible, as a result of his extractive talents. Until his last breath, his commitment to imposing the maximum sentence for acts of injustice will continue without abatement.

Forget about his brain—we will just take that for granted. That is not what made him successful. These three attributes—integrity, passion and energy—combined to make him hated by those who sought to tread on "lesser" human beings and to cause rejoicing among those who had a sense of fairness.

While Joe is not nearly so old, these words spoken by Oliver Wendell Holmes on his ninetieth birthday bring Joe to mind:

"The riders in a race do not stop short when they reach the goal. There is a little finishing canter before coming to a standstill. There is time to hear the kind voices of friends and to say to one's self: 'The work is done.' But just as one says that, the answer comes: 'The race is over, but the work never is done while the power to work remains.'"

HARRY M. REASONER
Former Managing Partner, Vinson & Elkins

I had heard of Joe Jamail when I was a student at Rice University, at the end of the 1950s. Sunset Boulevard, the northern boundary of the Rice campus for many years, had two beautiful oak trees in islands in the boulevard.

One evening a drunken driver ran squarely into the middle of one of the trees in a one-car accident. Joe sued for the driver. I thought the tree was a heavy favorite in the trial. Joe, however, persuaded the jury it was the tree's fault. The city both paid damages and cut down the trees.

Years later, when I became a trial lawyer myself, that case came to epitomize to me the dedication, creativity, and immensely powerful advocacy that Joe brings to bear on a client's behalf. He recovered a large sum for his injured client in a case most lawyers would never have taken.

His accomplishments and fame grew steadily, but I did not really get to know him until 1985, when he obtained the $10.53-billion-dollar verdict in *Pennzoil v. Texaco*. Anticipating an all-out assault on the verdict by Texaco, Joe enlisted a number of lawyers, including me, to assist in the appeal, in addition to the lawyers from Baker Botts, with whom he had led the case.

It was a diverse group: Louis Loss, Harvard professor and father of modern federal securities law; Larry Tribe, eminent Supreme Court advocate and constitutional scholar at Harvard; Arthur Liman, senior partner at Paul Weiss in New York and among the top handful of trial lawyers in the city; W. James Kronzer, dean of the Texas appellate bar and a brilliant advocate; and several other prominent lawyers and retired judges from across Texas.

The talent assembled was immense, but so were the egos.

Joe was a splendid leader, making each member of the team feel he had great and special value, listening, but firmly deciding at each juncture when decisions had to be made. Often, great patience was required. On our final brief to the Court of Appeals, Joe had to sit at a table with lawyers from two firms involved in writing it and decide, page by page, what the final language would be. I have worked with many large groups of talented lawyers. I have never seen one better led. We successfully fought off Texaco in the United States Supreme Court, the Texas Court of Appeals, the Texas Supreme Court, the Texas legislature, and the U.S. Bankruptcy Court.

After Pennzoil was settled in 1988, I had the great good fortune to work with Joe on a number of cases. He has taught me a great deal about the law and about life. He has not let the law narrow him, as so many do. He reads omnivorously and remains in genuine touch with all walks of life. He is not merely a great lawyer. He is a compassionate citizen who cares about society in general and his fellow man individually. He is a great and interesting human being.

Perhaps my favorite memory of our trials was in Midland, where we represented Home Savings Association, a savings and loan controlled by a group that manufactured trailer homes, sold trailer homes, and financed trailer homes through it. The plaintiff, American Bankers' Insurance, was a company that had made a fortune selling credit life on the trailer homes. It was persuaded by Home Savings to write mortgage insurance on each trailer so that its loan was paid off in the event of a default.

Banker's claimed our salesmen were giving $100 down payments to people on the street, so they could sell a trailer and then claim the mortgage insurance. There were some 17,000 claims by Home Savings for defaulted loans against Bankers under the mortgage policy. Bankers sought to declare all the claims void because of Home Savings' alleged fraudulent conduct in either selling defective trailers or selling them to people who could not afford them. We counter-claimed for the full amount of mortgage insurance.

Early in its case, Bankers put on the stand an attractive, matronly African-American grandmother. We were taking turns handling the cross-examination of witnesses, and Joe was to cross her. She told in a clear and dignified way of spending her life savings on one of Home Savings affiliate's trailers. She told of trying to raise her grandchildren in it with the roof leaking, the toilet not working, the flooring breaking through when she stepped on it. She told, with tears streaming silently down her cheeks, of calling repeatedly to get her warranty honored, of being told no one was in the office, and walking five miles to find the man responsible sitting there and refusing to take her calls.

As I watched her testify, I thought, What a nightmare; how could this woman possibly be cross-examined without making our client look worse than it already did in the eyes of the jury? I looked forward to seeing Joe attempt it.

As the lady finished her direct testimony, Joe leaned over and whispered to me, "I'm leaving, my boy, you can cross-examine her. We'll see what kind of lawyer you are. Good luck."

He walked out of the courtroom. I then made one of the worst tactical mistakes of my career. I stood up to cross-examine. Joe ultimately negotiated a brilliant settlement during trial, worth some $75 million.

DARRELL ROYAL
National Championship Football Coach, University of Texas

I had heard of Joe Jamail but had never met him until a Texas alumnus called, wanting to play a practical joke on Joe. The alum knew I was trying to recruit a fine young lineman named Bobby Wuensch, and it turned out that his mother, Opal, had gone all through school with Joe's wife, Lee, at San Marcos Academy in San Marcos, Texas.

I didn't care much about the joke, but I cared about recruiting Bobby. The alum gave me the Jamails' phone number but emphasized that I should contact Lee and not go through Joe, who was a great booster for Texas and our football team. He repeated himself, "Make sure you don't go through Joe." The idea, I guess, was that it would drive Joe nuts to have the Texas football coach talking to his wife and not him.

I got to their home in midafternoon and then Joe showed up from work. He and I wound up talking for hours in the kitchen, and I remember thinking, "This is my kind of guy." We have been great and solid "pod-nuhs" ever since.

There isn't anyone out there who is his equal for unselfishness and compassion. I've called him from all over the country for advice, and no one is better at putting thoughts together, or words.

He has amassed considerable wealth, and entirely from his own talent and labors, not from investments or stocks or real estate. Few have shared the fruits of their success so generously or joyfully. Joe and Lee contributed many millions to their alma mater, the University of Texas, and the field at Darrell K. Royal–Memorial Stadium is named after him.

I have always felt a bit embarrassed about having my name up there, but I'm pleased to share the marquee with Joe.

After he underwent heart surgery in 1998, he asked his surgeon, Denton Cooley, a one-time Texas basketball star, what he could do for him.

"Well, Joe," said Dr. Cooley, "you might think about giving us some money."

He wrote out a check for $10 million to the Texas Heart Institute.

Somehow, Willie Nelson and I became a part of his Pennzoil triumph by showing up on his doorstep the night before he was to make his closing argument. I didn't even know he was working on this huge case.

Willie called and said, "We ought to fly down to Houston and see Joe." Willie had his own plane then. When we knocked on the door, Joe was in his den, preparing the remarks that would convince the jury to award Pennzoil a verdict of over $10 billion.

I don't have any recollection of what we talked about that night. I know Joe didn't want to talk about the law and I didn't want to talk about football, so I guess we just talked about life and country music, which are sometimes the same thing. Mostly, we sat and listened to Willie Nelson sing and play his guitar.

Some stories have said we stayed all night, but we actually left well before midnight. I do know that Joe says it was just about the best way any lawyer ever found to shape up his closing argument.

RICK GOLDBERG *Tri-Coastal Legal Technologies*

Editor's note: Goldberg, whose firm was among the first to provide high-tech courtroom support, prepared this text as a lecture for law students. He decided to focus on a lawyer who, for all his success, was open to new concepts.

Famed. Flamboyant. Legendary. Such words inevitably precede any reference to Houston attorney Joe Jamail.

Of course, big actions breed big words: Jamail's $11 billion jury award against Texaco. His 200-plus favorable verdicts. His willingness decades ago to stand up to Joe McCarthy's henchman Roy Cohn and, more recently, to confront Texas Attorney General Dan Morales for allegedly demanding political donations in exchange for a spot on the state's Big Tobacco legal team.

Jamail has donated tens of millions of dollars to Texas

hospitals and universities. Even the University of Texas football field is named after the guy. No wonder *Texas Monthly* pronounced him "Lawyer of the Century."

And yet, having provided trial support to Jamail on two cases now—the *Kendall Montgomery v. John O'Quinn* "slugfest" (as the *Houston Chronicle* phrased it) and a medical malpractice case that recently settled (*Mackenzie Dunford v. Bayou City Medical*), I've developed a parallel theory.

What makes a lawyer legendary? Big successes, sure. But also the little things: the tactics and habits that may not scream across the headlines but that those of us behind the scenes marvel at as we watch them add up to big wins.

Assembling a strong team

Let's face it, the courtroom's no place for shrinking violets. Star attorneys develop reputations for healthy egos. And yet Jamail has impressed me as a lawyer who, despite his self-confidence in the limelight, surrounds himself with people of exemplary competence. He's smart enough to know there are a lot of other smart people out there; any personal hankerings for a starring role never take precedence over his goal of winning. In the Dunford case, Jamail ceded center stage to his co-counsel, the very organized and insightful Janet Hansen. Hansen gave the opening and directed the examination of certain key witnesses; she knew every line of testimony and every medical record cold. No wonder this partnership has been so successful over the past twenty years.

Attorney Fred Hagans, of Hagans, Bobb & Burdine, collaborated with Jamail on the Kendall-Montgomery case, and he echoes my observations on Jamail's teamwork. "This was the first time I worked with Joe, and I was impressed that he would listen to new and different ideas, evaluate them, and then decide whether to incorporate them or not. He didn't make quick decisions; he was always open-minded to what other members of the team had to contribute."

Once Jamail hires you, he lets you do your job. He's not a micromanager or a control freak; he knows where his expertise lies. He might tell me he wants to show a damage summary tomorrow morning, but then he'll go off to do what he does best, leaving us to do what we do best.

Making other people look and feel good

There are no "little people" to Joe Jamail. Whether you're running a multimedia presentation, keeping order in the court, or cross-examining his expert, Jamail honors your role in the proceedings. Clerks, bailiffs, legal assistants: all are made to feel good about themselves. Jamail is courteous, he makes genuine eye contact, he doesn't rush you. Juries appreciate his charm, and as a non-lawyer who has spent thousands of hours in courtrooms, I can safely assert that he is in a league of his own on this front.

In particular, Jamail excels at presenting his experts. Some of his medical witnesses in the Dunford trial had fifty- to seventy-page curriculum vitae. A detailed recitation of their achievements would have bored the jurors and possibly turned them off. On the other hand, the jury needed to be convinced of the witnesses' credibility.

Jamail's strategy? He directed us to scan the experts' entire vitae along with the other trial exhibits. Then, during the trial, we showed the jury the electronic pages on our eight-by-ten-foot rear-projection screen, but with no single page appearing for more than one or two seconds. This was long enough for the jury to see the key heading—Medical Licenses—and its two pages of entries before we moved on to Publications and its seventy-eight numbered entries. And so on.

The jury sat in impressed silence—and they got the expert's picture, in minutes, rather than hours. "Those two minutes of silence," said the Hon. Russell P. Austin (Harris County Probate Court. No 1), "were the best credibility-builders for any expert witness I have ever seen."

Then, before intimidation could set in, Jamail's first question to the witness went something like this: "Now I know, Doctor, that you're not one to toot your own horn. But you're world-renowned in this field, aren't you?" He gave this extremely accomplished and famous individual an opportunity to be humble, a regular guy whom the jurors could relate to.

Love of the sport

Like certain baseball players who appreciate their game's rich past, Jamail boasts a deep understanding of the history of the legal system, and he understands his place within it. His strategic preparedness reminds me of another legendary figure, Hall of Fame football coach Bill Walsh. Walsh would begin every San Francisco Forty-Niners game with his first thirty plays pre-scripted. Regardless of what happened during the opening minutes—fumbles, interceptions, touchdowns—he stuck to his game plan.

Jamail is equally prepared when he enters the courtroom. He and co-counsel Hagans met every day during the month leading up to the Kendall-Montgomery trial, discussing their order of witnesses and the agenda for each. "Joe is not just a 'big picture' guy," Hagans says. "He knows every question he is going to ask. We fine-tuned and tweaked all the way up to opening statements."

Also, because so few cases nowadays go to trial, fewer and fewer lawyers, even those with vast experience with major firms, regularly get to argue a case before a jury. When it comes to courtrooms, Jamail has been there many a time, and it shows.

An openness to technology

Few lawyers still hover over their secretaries pecking out fifth or sixth drafts on IBM Selectrics. But how many attorneys really keep abreast of the strategic advantages technology can offer? Though born in 1925, and thus having left law school with little more equipment than a legal pad and a pencil, the seventy-six-year-old Jamail doesn't shy away from cutting-edge technology that can benefit him in the courtroom.

For example, in the Dunford case, thirty-one depositions were videotaped. We then digitized each video and synchronized it to witnesses' ASCII transcript. After Jamail and Hansen created a list of the line and page designations they wanted to offer, we imported the list into our editing software and immediately determined the duration of each witness's examination. As is usually the case, the first cut was too long.

However, editing the video down wasn't an enormous obstacle for us. Because we had digitized the video in advance, we were able to quickly delete some designations and substantially trim the total run time. The entire process took about two hours.

An attorney using less sophisticated technology would have still been slumped in their Barcalounger with a bound deposition in one hand and a remote control in the other (and a pack of Rolaids in their shirt pocket). Meanwhile, Jamail's team was immediately able to begin fine-tuning their experts' testimony. Later, we maintained maximum spontaneity going into the courtroom. Whenever testimony became irrelevant or was ruled inadmissible, I could edit out that portion of the video within seconds right there on my laptop. You couldn't do this with a VHS cassette.

Even judges—or perhaps judges most of all—appreciate attorneys' skillful use of technology. Says Judge

Austin: "With so much at stake, I'm surprised I don't see more attorneys taking advantage of technology to speed up the proceedings and make their cases easier for juries to understand."

Proving liability and damages in a trice

There is a reason the *20-20s* and the *Sixty Minutes* news shows limit their exposés to ten- or twelve-minute segments. Any longer and they'd lose their audience. Yet how many attorneys continue to torment juries with one forty-to-sixty-minute videotape of a witness after another?

Joe Jamail has an amazing ability to key in on witnesses' crucial testimony. In the Dunford case, we put on twenty-six witnesses in six days, twenty-one of them via videotape. When the video witness referred to an exhibit, the exhibit was pre-linked to appear alongside the witness, thus allowing the jury to view exactly what the witness was discussing. Jamail would present a witness by video for ten minutes, establish liability and damages, and move on to the next witness.

"His ability to reduce the depositions down to the critical nine to twelve minutes was the best I've ever seen," Judge Austin said later. "When they told me they were going to play five and a half hours of straight video one day, I thought the jury was going to lose interest and become fatigued. As it turned out, it was the most productive day of the trial and the jury never lost focus."

Equally impressive was Jamail's ability to end his witness examination in a strategic place. Each new witness seemed to pick up on a comment or theme at which the previous witness had left off. An engaging narrative developed. Also, because many of the witnesses were called adverse, the defense declined to cross-examine them until later, knowing they would get but one shot. In effect, Jamail prevented the defense from interrupting his momentum.

Knowing when—and when not—to show your cards

Prior to the Dunford trial, we created a powerful, full-blown multimedia presentation in preparation for mediation. It included fifty to sixty slides showcasing key documents, critical testimony, and compelling timelines and charts. Such presentations are usually an excellent strategy for mediation. You educate the other side's insurance representatives and/or general counsel as to the strength of your case and in the process attempt to convince them that by settling they might spare themselves a catastrophic verdict.

However, the day before mediation, Jamail became convinced that the other side was not about to settle, regardless of the strength of our case. Though we'd committed extensive resources in creating a very persuasive presentation, Jamail opted not to show it. Why tip our hand, he asked?

As Jamail predicted, we went to trial. Prior to putting on their case and after we put on twenty-six witnesses, the defense sized up the proceedings and both parties settled. Because Jamail had exercised restraint, he left the defendants wondering what was coming next. Evidently, they realized they ought not to take a chance.

Texas is a big state that produces many personalities. Many aim for the big coup—the largest jury award ever, for example—and may appreciate the spin value of a grand gesture. But few, I suspect, reach legendary status without genuine qualities and abilities that set them apart. When you watch Joe Jamail in action, whether behind the scenes or in his milieu—the courtroom—you can't help but feel that you are witnessing one for the history books.

This actually happened. It is a snippet from the transcript of a trial invoving a wrongful death suit. An attorney for the defendant is questioning the pathologist about an autopsy:

Q. Do you recognize the person in Plaintiff's Exhibit 8?
A. Yes. It is Mr. Edgington.
Q. Do you recall approximately the time you examined the body of Mr. Edgington at the Rose Chapel?
A. It was in the evening. The autopsy started at about 8:30 P.M.
Q. And Mr. Edgington was dead at that time, is that correct?
A. No, you dumb asshole. He was sitting up on the table wondering why I was doing an autopsy.

I believe it is essential for a lawyer to enter every trial with controlled anger and a sense of humor. I did not lose either one, at least not for long, in the Pennzoil case.

He should also, whenever possible, avoid asking really stupid questions, like the one asked in this.

JOSEPH D. JAMAIL

BORN: October 19, 1925, Houston, Texas

PREPARATORY EDUCATION: University of Texas (B.A., 1950)

LEGAL EDUCATION: University of Texas (J.D., 1953)

ADMITTED TO THE BAR: August 1952, Texas

HOUSTON BAR ASSOCIATION

STATE BAR OF TEXAS (Chairman, Grievance Committee, 1963, District 22; Chairman, Town Hall Task Force, 1973–74)

AMERICAN BAR ASSOCIATION

Fellow, American College of Trial Lawyers

Fellow, International Academy of Trial Lawyers

Inner Circle of Advocates

Advocate, American Board of Trial Advocates

Fellow, International Society of Barristers

Fellow, International Academy of Law and Science

Fellow, Council of Law and Science

Association of Trial Lawyers of America

World Association of Lawyers

Philosophical Society of Texas

The University of Texas Ex-Students' Association, Life Member

The University of Texas School of Law created "The Joseph D. Jamail Centennial Chair in Law and Advocacy"

Recipient of the 1989 Jurisprudence Award by The Anti-Defamation League of B'nai B'rith

Grand Marshall of the Martin Luther King Day Parade, Houston, Texas, 1989

Recipient of the Southern Trial Lawyers Association 1993 War Horse Award

Recipient of the 1993 Brotherhood Award of the National Conference of Christians and Jews

Recipient of the 1996 University of Texas School of Law Outstanding Alumnus Award

University of Texas has designated the Jessie Jones Hall at the Law School as "The Joseph D. Jamail Center for Legal Research"

Recipient of the 1993 Houston Texas Exes award

Recipient of the 1996 University of Texas Distinguished Alumnus Award

Honorary member Order of Barristers, University of Texas

Named by *Texas Monthly* magazine (12/99) "The Lawyer of the Century" and named "King of Torts" by *Washington Post, Chicago Tribune,* and other publications

Featured in recent book *America's Top Trial Lawyers,* by Donald E. Vinson, copyright 1994 by Prentice Hall Law & Business

Named one of the country's top trial lawyers by most credible legal publications

Represented a client who received the largest jury verdict in the history of law: *Pennzoil v. Texaco*—$11,120,000,000

Represented a client who received the largest cash award at the time in the history of tort law—*Coates v. Remington Arms*

Represented a client who received a verdict and judgment for $560 million in a negligence and fraud case: *United States National Bank of Galveston, et. al v. Coopers & Lybrand, et. al*

Has been lead counsel in over two hundred personal injury cases where recovery, either by verdict or settlement, was in excess of $1 million

Has won over $12 billion in jury verdicts and over $13 billion in verdicts and settlements

Guest lecturer at many law schools throughout the country, including the University of Texas

Named "Trial Lawyer of the Century" by California Trial Lawyers, *Texas Monthly,* and others

Tried three cases which resulted in manufacturer product recalls—Remington 600, Honda All Terrain Three-Wheel Vehicle, prescription drug Parlodel